The World According To Michael

Michael Lightweaver
lightweave@aol.com

Mountain Light Publishing
PO Box 18909
Asheville, NC. 28814, USA
www.mtnlightsanctuary.com

Copyright @ 2014
by Michael Lightweaver
All Rights Reserved

Contents

* The Big Question   5
* It's All Just Curriculum   6
* Is That Really True?   8
* Does it Grow Corn?   10
* Your Ultimate Objective   11
* The Secret Of Happiness   12
* Prisoners of History   14
* You Are Going To Die   15
* Mini-Me / Maxi-Me   15
* Sex & Death   16
* On Being Gay   19
* Chop Wood Carry Water   21
* So What's the Purpose of it all?   22
* Organized Religion   23
* Falling in love   26
* The Preposition Oracle   28
* In Every Seeming Adversity   29
* It Just Do What It Do   30
* Dog Track theory   32
* What If?   33
* As Within, So Without   34
* Dealing With Problems   35
* What is Wisdom?   36
* Two Roads   37
* Predicting The Future   39
* The Warehouse of Possibilities   40

Additional Writings

* The Galactic Fairytale   43
* A Message From Big Mama   46
* Are You Suffering From PMT   48
* Decisive Moments   50
* The Musings Of A Minor Prophet   56
* My Journey   58
* Reflections on the Middle East   74
* The Ultimate Guru   76
* Where Is The Gift?   78
* God in Drag   79
* The Keys To Eden   85
* Kissing Frogs   89
* The Bible Says That?   91

Acknowledgements

Many people have passed through my life and each of them have touched me in different ways and contributed to who I am. My parents and sister, my wife of forty six years, four children and eight grandchildren; my lovers, my extended family of friends and coworkers, the many guests who have visited the Sanctuary – and yes, even the rare adversary; each of you have contributed to my being who I am and the way I see the world. To each of you I owe a debt of gratitude, for 'my world' is really the result of the many ways you touched my life.

Preface

This book is really being written for my great, great, great grandchildren who will be living into the 22nd century and whom I may never know. I remember as a child hearing scattered stories of my great grandfather, Anderson Hewitt: of how he fought in the civil war, how he was educated for his time in a world of peasant farmers in Kentucky. How he used to go out in the fields and "make speeches to the Black folks." From the little I could piece together, he was apparently an abolitionist, which said to me that he marched to the tune of a different drummer than most of his peers and family in southern Kentucky.

Perhaps it was for that reason that he was always my secret hero. I also remember as a child an old trunk in the basement of our home that had some yellowed family ledgers and sepia photos of stern looking ancestors from the 1800's. As I looked into their eyes, even as a youth, I wondered about their stories. What had they experienced? What hardships had they endured? What did they think? What was their view of the world? At the time I remembered that the greatest gift that I could imagine would be to sit down with them, hear their stories and see the world through their eyes and experience.

So this is why I am writing this book; as a gift to you, my descendants; a gift that I would have loved to receive from my own ancestors. It is my attempt to give you a window into my world, back in 2014 and let you see what I thought and what made me tick.

And to others who may read this, perhaps you will find something of value – or perhaps not. As one of my favorite authors – Anthony Robbins - says, when he stops in the middle of a passionate motivational speech; "Is any of this true? I have no idea, but it is a helpful way of looking at things."

As I sit here, in 2014, wondering about you, my descendants, I can hardly imagine what kind of world you live in. During my lifetime I have seen the advent of television, tape recorders, personal computers, the internet, digital photos, cell phones and much, much more. I remember getting our first television when I was six years old. All of the TV's at that time were only black and white so my dad bought a made-for-television colored plastic sheet to tape over the screen. The top was blue and the bottom was green – for sky and grass – since most of the shows were cowboy and Indian movies! I also remember the pride I had when I bought my first tape recorder in the early 1970s and the first boxy little Macintosh computer in 1992, starting with floppy drives, zip disks, wallet size external hard drives and finally the tiny flash drives – all of which may seem terribly primitive to you in the 22nd Century. With the technological changes I have seen in my lifetime I can't even imagine your world.

However, when I compare my world with that of my distant ancestors, in spite of the technological changes, I see very little change in human nature. Here, in the early part of the 21st century, we still have wars, starvation, dictators, torture and terrorism, racism, sexism, religious fanaticism, injustice and vast gaps between the very poor and the very rich. Though supposedly we have the tools and resources to solve many of our challenges, we don't seem to have the collective will. Our technological advances have far out raced the development of human consciousness, which seems to cling to our Neanderthal past.

Over the course of our lives, we develop a story about who we are. I call it our myth. It is built from our experiences, our beliefs, our self-concept and our relationships. It is the story we tell others and ourselves. It may or may not be true or factual, but it is our truth and what frames our lives.

Here is my myth. I came to the planet this time around on assignment. The latter part of the 20th and the first part of the 21st century marks a major turning point on the Earth. A new era is being birthed and many have come at this time to play a midwifery role in that birthing. Needless to say, I also have a ton of personal work to do – karma if you will – this time around.

But this trip also involves planetary transformational work. That work has taken many forms over the course of years, which I won't go into at this point. I only mention it as background info for what follows and to give you a better idea of who your great, great, great grandfather was.

Introduction
My paternal grandfather died three months after I was born, so I never really got to know him. I only had one or two stories from my sister, his first grandchild, speaking of her warm memories. As I look back now, I realize how

little I really knew any of my grandparents and to some extent my own parents who were still alive when I was in my 50's.

Each of us is a living story with rich experiences that are too often lost when we leave the physical realm. When you are young you never think to ask for those stories and by the time you are much older, you have established such a fixed role with each family member that you seldom traverse the invisible boundaries with probing questions that could bring forth those stories.

The book is divided into two sections, the first of which was written in the winter of 2014. The second section, 'Additional Writings,' was written over a period of 20 years starting in 1990. You will find that there is a great deal of overlap and some repetition centered on certain primary themes, which represents the growth, and clarification of my understanding of life over two decades.

What you are about to read is part one of my own story. It is the story of the way I see the world. I don't pretend that any of it is "true." All I can say with some certainty is that, after nearly 70 years of experience on this planet I have found that it is a way of seeing the world that works reasonably well for me. It is the world according to Michael.

The Big Question

Anthony Robbins also says that our lives are determined by our questions. For me the big question has always been "Why Are We Here?" What is this all about? Are we here just to experience the joys and pain of childhood; the challenges of puberty and our teen years, school – endless school – followed by the fun and fiction of relationships, family, kids, mortgage, jobs, debt, old age and death? Is life just a bouncing between ecstasy and agony?

It took me about 50 years to figure this one out, or at least to come to some conclusions that made sense and gave meaning to the whole comedy/tragedy drama of human existence.

It began with what I started learning in the early 1980's when I created the Human Potential Institute: a clinical hypnosis practice in Nashville, Tennessee (USA). In the course of using hypnosis to find the source of a clients concern in some event or situation in their childhood, I would occasionally do regressions. Needless to say, it came as a big surprise when individuals would sometimes regress back to a supposed past life – especially when they did not believe in reincarnation.

At the time I had no special belief about the subject, as it was not a part of my Christian upbringing. But as it began to happen on a regular basis I launched into a lot of reading to get a better understanding of what it could all mean. From personal experience with clients as well as historical research into early Christian teachings, exploring other cultural and religious beliefs, and common sense born from observing nature, I came to see that we don't have to get it all done in one life. Each of our lives is but a very brief chapter in a very long book.

If this is true, then what is the plot? Gradually I came to see that it is really all about "soul growth."

Imagine the waves of the ocean crashing upon seaside cliffs. The ocean spray is made of a million droplets, all of them individual manifestations of the ocean that exist for a moment of time before returning to the ocean. It is the oceans way of experiencing its individuality in a moment of time and carrying that experience back to its source.

Now put that in slow motion. The wave crashes upon the shore and we are each a droplet of the whole, existing for an instant in time and space, experiencing a moment of amnesia and believing in our individuality and our various dramas until we return to the Great Source waiting for the next ocean wave. Each time we crash upon the rocks we give birth to new experiences and each time we return, we carry that experience back to the great ocean we call God. In other words we are all aspects of Divine Presence experiencing itself. At the same time, all of our experience contributes to our own soul growth over many, many life times.

It's All Just Curriculum

If this is true, then ultimately all of our experiences in life are just curriculum. Some of it is pleasant and a great deal of it is unpleasant, but it is all instructive to those who have ears to hear and eyes to see. It has been my experience that our curriculum falls roughly into four categories: finance, romance, our bodies and our egos.

You can go searching for a guru in a remote cave in India or seek out a shaman in the mountains, but in truth, the Creator gave each of us these four fundamental teachers.

Lets start with money as an example. They say that money can't buy you happiness. This is probably true, but it is equally true that the lack of money can certainly bring you a great deal of pain, stress or sadness. Anyone who has experienced this understands.

From the time you leave home as a child or youth until the time that you lose direct control of your finances as a result of an accident, illness or old age – you will be dealing with money and learning all that it has to teach you. You will have the opportunity to learn about spending, budgeting, generosity, greed, honesty, integrity, how to manage with too little and how to manage wisely with too much.

Your money and how you handle it will give you an opportunity to learn a great deal about yourself, your values, your goals, your discernment, your self-image. And how you use it will give others a clear snapshot of who you are; your strengths, your weaknesses, your beliefs, what you really value in life. Money can become a great mirror for you to take a close look at yourself, seeing what you like about yourself and what you may want to change.

And then there are relationships. Our human relationships begin with our parents or early care givers. I ascribe to the idea that we do in fact choose our parents before we pop in for any given incarnation. They become our initial teachers – not just in terms of information – but also in terms of experience. Our early experience with parents can give us a good hint as to the level of difficulty of the curriculum we have chosen for this incarnation.

The more issues you have with your parents, the richer the curriculum and opportunities you have for soul growth. For a moment, step away from the blame game related to what they did or didn't do, and pretend – just pretend – that all of this occurred as a part of the curriculum that you chose.

I'm not asking you to believe it. Just pretend because this will give you a new set of glasses through which you can view the situation and open you to new learnings. As long as we are locked into the blame game and our victim mentality, we limit our vision for seeing the bigger picture.

This can also be said about our third piece of curriculum; our bodies. Like money, your body is going to be with you all of your life. You will have to deal with it as a teenager, whether it is facial blemishes, unruly hair or the dramatic changes of puberty. Your body will be constantly talking to you and seeking your attention in a thousand different ways. As you get older and wage the battle against weight, sagging, wrinkling and the gradual breakdown of various functions, your body may demand more and more of your attention. And then there are those who experience illness or accidents in which the body suddenly requires 100% of your attention. But guess what? It is all just curriculum. A great deal of it related to the body, is unpleasant but oh so instructive.

Ego. I remember a talk by Ram Dass in which he said that we are all in "somebody training." A big part of our human training has to do with individuation; coming to see ourselves as individuals distinctly different than others. In this piece of curriculum, the Ego becomes our guru. It likes nothing better than to feel special and it can do it in a thousand different ways. Sports, academics, trophies, degrees, the biggest house, the most expensive car, the most popular, the most friends, the most bling, the most spiritually enlightened. All of them are egos way of making you feel special, better, or at least different than others. From the moment we wake up in the morning until the last moment before falling asleep, we are experiencing the curriculum of one or more of these four gurus – and most of it unconsciously.

If we were able to stand back and see our daily dramas from a larger perspective we would begin to recognize the rich curriculum we have created for ourselves or at least attracted into our lives. And if we start seeing the same drama occurring over and over in our lives, with different actors, then this is a clear cue as to the primary issues we need to work on.

Is That Really True?

One of the things that I have noticed is that most of our lives and virtually all of our actions are based on assumptions and not facts. Perhaps this is the reason that so many different people come to such different conclusions about any specific event or situation.

Let me give an example. Recently a major storm pounded New York City and the coast of New Jersey. We could consider that a fact in as much as it was verifiable by those who experienced it directly and those who learned about it via images in the media.

There seemed to be common agreement that it did happen. So we can consider the storm and it's damage to be a fact. This fact, however, spun off a host of assumptions as to the cause of the storm. For example, a TV evangelist might sincerely attribute it to being God's wrath because of the state's approval of gay marriage.

The climatologist would say, unequivocally, that it was the result of global warming, while the conspiracy theorist might lay the blame at the feet of the government or the global elite with their hidden agendas. For each of them, their own understanding of the cause is 'true.'

The point is this. Each of their interpretations is no more than assumptions based on their paradigm or worldview. Each of us have a set of beliefs defined by our personal experience, religious background, political perspective, ethnic experience, family background, social status, culture and the era we live in. All of our experiences, both individually and collectively are viewed through a certain set of colored glasses defined by these filters, and the conclusions drawn may or may not be true. They are simply our interpretation of the facts.

Why is this important? It is important because we live our lives and handle our affairs largely based on these assumptions, which may or may not be valid and our assumption-based actions may lead to devastating results both personally and collectively.

Let us consider a couple of examples. Each of us may know of a friend or family member – or perhaps from personal experience – where we have seen playing out in full force the old adage "love is blind." You see your friend has fallen in love with an individual and suddenly becomes totally blinded to all of the other persons flaws and faults, which you can see clearly. A few years down the road, when the honeymoon is over and at the end of a bitter divorce, your friend has come to the opposite conclusion. Now the former lover can do no right.

Every act, however positive, is interpreted negatively. In both cases, there is zero objectivity because in the first case, all actions are viewed through the rose colored glasses of romantic infatuation while in the second case, all actions are interpreted through the gray mist of disappointment, anger and perhaps hatred. In neither case are the actual facts considered as to what was said or done. And even something that appeared to be positive to an objective outsider would be attributed to malevolent motives by the offended party.

This is dangerous enough on a personal level and the prisons and cemeteries are filled with the victims of such assumptions, which were based on beliefs rather than facts.

At a national and international level, these assumptions lead to war, genocide, racism, sexism, starvation, torture and all of the other symptoms of human dysfunction.

History is full of such examples but perhaps the most recent, in my era, is the USA invasion of Iraq based on an assumption that this country had weapons of mass destruction. A 'fact' sold to the American public, which later proved to be a false but still contributed to the death of thousands of innocent people and ongoing turmoil in the region.

So, whether in your personal relationships or whether any individual or group is trying to 'sell you a bill of goods' or convince you of a certain fact, look at their paradigm – their world view – their set of beliefs. Learn to separate fact from fantasy; fact from assumption; fact from wishing and hoping. Bottom line, learn to think for yourself.

Does It Grow Corn?

I was once asked what inscription I would want for the headstone of my grave. Since cremation is my preferred manner of disposal, I don't anticipate such an inscription. However, if I did, I think it would simply be the question, "Does It Grow Corn?" As I have indicated before, our lives are defined by our questions. For most people, the first question is "Is it true?" While this is a valid question for some things, such as someone trying to sell you a questionable item, there are many things that we cannot know the truth of. For example, I have done many past life regressions through the use of hypnosis. The first question that many people ask, after returning from their inward journey into another life is "was that really a past life?" The truth is, in most cases the facts, such as they are, are not verifiable. And frankly, I'm not concerned with the truth of it, any more than the truth of this philosophy as compared to that philosophy. The valid question, for me, is not whether is it true but does it work, serve or help a person. In other words, does it grow corn?

I heard this saying from one of my Native American elders. The indigenous spiritual path was of necessity a practical one. If your belief system doesn't 'grow corn' then you don't eat. If you don't eat, then you die. Period. So, in spite of being a dreamer and visionary by nature, I have always been practical in my approach. I like what works, as long as it is in alignment with my basic values.

Unfortunately, human beings are more inclined to be governed by their beliefs, assumptions and emotions rather than by the practical application of what works. Again, let us consider some examples.

When faced with a medical situation the first inclination is to find a remedy, often prescribed by a professional. If we find that the remedy doesn't work, do we increase the dose, change medications or venture further afield to consider other alternatives? How often do we stop to ask why we are experiencing the health challenge? What is the real source, physical or otherwise, of the problem? We consider the how (remedy) but seldom the why (source of the problem).

The same is true with personal relationships. When we are in conflict with an individual, our brain often takes a vacation and our response is totally emotional.

When we respond emotionally with a certain action and that action bears no fruit, too often we simply intensify the same response.

We double our efforts in how to deal with the situation rather than pausing to consider the why of it. Once we discover the why, then our parameter of possible solutions increases. But this requires the objective proactive operation of the brain rather than the reactive operation of the emotions.

An international example is the ongoing and seemingly endless conflict in "the Land of Jerusalem" between the Jewish and Palestinian people. It seems that the strategy is "if it doesn't work, do more of it." Duhhhhh....' This approach is based on a few basic ideas: Each party contends that they are right and the others are wrong. Each would rather punish or have revenge on the other rather than find a solution. The ruling belief is that if our approach doesn't work, we will do more of it rather than consider alternatives. This of course is not true of all Israelis or Palestinians but it is the governing principle of those in power on each side. I only use Israel and Palestine as examples that most people are familiar with. But I have noticed that this is the way that virtually all nations and governments operate – not to mention individuals (yes, each of us). We have progressed very little beyond the kindergarten playground in our personal and international relations.

I'm not saying that it is either right or wrong since after all, it is our collective curriculum as a species. However, I have noticed that it doesn't grow corn, in terms of creating a peaceful, prosperous, free and just world.

So the next time you contemplate a decision or action, ask yourself "will this grow corn" in terms of my ultimate objective.

The Ultimate Objective

And what is the ultimate objective in life? We have considered the ultimate question, now lets look at the ultimate objective. What is your bottom line? What is it that you really want in life? What does it all boil down to, really? I have found that most people just want to be happy or to experience joy. It is a feeling or an experience. This seems to be the common denominator that unites us all regardless of where we live, our age, our social status or any other of the categories that divide us. We all want to be happy or to experience joy.

The differences begin to show up with the conditions we consider necessary to experience happiness. For most of us there are the basics of food, water, shelter, security.

The next tier might be personal freedom, love, peace of mind, self-esteem, etc. But beyond these, the conditions become more personal. For some it is a certain income, a certain kind of house, automobile or lifestyle, travel, a university degree, personal power, fame – the list can go on and on, ad infinitum. The longer the list of conditions that we base our happiness upon, the further we push it away. This is the reason that sages throughout history taught that simplicity or non-attachment are the foundation of happiness.

What I have noticed both with others, and myself is that – however fun goals are to set and aspire to – their attainment brings nothing more than a momentary sense of satisfaction and then we are off in pursuit of the next one.

The reason I bring this up is to challenge you to look at all of the things you want in life – the things that you think will make you happy. Trust me, they won't. While I admit that the lack of them can indeed make you sad, having them will not bring lasting happiness.

Should we then not pursue our goals? No, I think the pursuit of goals is a great endeavor and certainly the experiences we have in this pursuit are excellent curriculum. All I am saying is that we should not burden their attainment with the expectation that they will bring us happiness – a moment of satisfaction perhaps – but not happiness.

So what will bring you authentic happiness? That is the second big question but one that we must each answer for our self. For me, it is compassion, gratitude and generosity – i.e. giving. But that is according to my own nature.

These things bring me core happiness. Mind you, I am a long way from perfecting either of them, but I find their pursuit and periodic attainment make my heart glow and my days fulfilled.

The Secret of Happiness
It is true. I have had a good deal of interesting experience in my seventy years. I have read a ton of books. I've fallen on the floor laughing and I have screamed and sobbed my heart out in pain. I have loved from the depths of my being and experienced both the agony and ecstasy of romance.

I have also spent countless hours sitting with others in their own pain, offering what little Guidance I had to give. From all of this I have gleaned perhaps an ounce of wisdom, and if not true wisdom, at least some understanding. The result has been that I have reached a few conclusions that, for the moment, seem to be true and satisfy me.

The secret of happiness has always been the holy grail of human pursuit. Perhaps that secret is different for each person. In my younger years I believed it was the attainment of goals – very often material ones – that would lead to happiness. But as I dutifully attained each of these goals I realized that they brought only a moment of satisfaction but no lasting happiness. Finally I came to realize that my true source of happiness was Gratitude and Generosity.

Regardless of our circumstances in life, we always have the choice of looking at those who have more or those who have less. Regardless of your station in life there will always be those who have more than you do; more money, more possessions, more fame, more love and better health. And there will always be those who have less. I found that my happiness largely depends on what I focus my attention on; whether I am in a state of gratitude for what I have or in perpetual angst for what I lack. It is that simple.

I have heard it said that studies have shown that pessimists are more realistic but optimists live longer and happier lives. At this stage in my life I can say that I am indeed happy. Yes, I still have worldly cares and challenges but I have found over the years, truth in the saying, "in every seeming adversity is the seed of an equal or greater benefit."

And in spite of any momentary unpleasantness or sense of loss, I have always found a gift; something to be grateful for. And not only this, but the simple habit of Gratitude – for even the simplest of things – creates a personal frequency of joy that builds upon itself and is self-perpetuating. Deep appreciation and gratitude have become the cornerstone of my joy.

A natural product of that Gratitude is Generosity. Living in a state of natural gratitude & deep appreciation for all that is, spontaneously opens the heart. As fear, anger, disappointment and hurt melt in the sunshine of Gratitude, the heart smiles and opens to a state of grace and giving.

There is a deep desire and joy that comes from giving to others from the bounty of one's own life; whether it is money, love, possessions or simply good vibes, and the more one gives in the spirit of grace, the greater the joy and happiness. And since life is a two way street and 'what goes around, comes around' that bounty returns in many forms and usually in greater measure. This is the second cornerstone of my joy.

Prisoners of History

Perhaps you have heard the old saying "Once burned, twice shy." A large part of human survival has resulted from our ability to learn from our past experience. We naturally try to avoid those situations in the past which have been perceived as a source of pain. This is true both individually and collectively. Let me explain.

Perhaps the most common is the disappointed love affair. Very often, when one is deeply disappointed in romance, one shies away from love altogether in an effort to never experience such pain again. The same is often true in other personal relationships. Once we have had a set of negative experiences with particular individuals, we live with the expectation that such experiences may continue into the future and we adjust our own behavior accordingly, once again in an effort to prevent additional pain.

At a social and international level, we see the same mechanism at work. Historical hatreds between ethnic groups, tribes, nations and religions are carried over from generation to generation like a genetic disease that is passed on from parents to children with no relief. The world is full of examples of this, the two of which come to mind most readily are the ongoing conflict in Northern Ireland and Israel and Palestine. The parties in each case demonize the other side and perpetuate this poison from generation to generation.

When you perceive that the other individual or group has been the source of your pain then it is quite natural to build internal and external defenses of protection. But in all cases, there is a price to pay, sometimes in the external physical world and sometimes internally at the frequency level of soul growth.

Here is the dilemma. Is it possible to be informed by our personal or collective history without becoming its prisoner? Can our past experience inform our present and influence our future without putting our present and future in 'lock down' or solitary confinement? And furthermore is it possible to change?

Does our present view of an individual or group account for the possibility that they can or have changed, grown or evolved? And what about ourselves; have we changed or evolved over the past decade? If so, do we want our friends and families to take this into account or are we satisfied that they continue to hold us hostage to their perception of who we were ten or twenty years ago.

14

And on a larger scale, with conflicts between groups, do we allow for the fact that everyone isn't the same, even if they belong to the same ethnic or religious group? In our effort to protect ourselves have we imprisoned ourselves in our own beliefs about another individual or group of people? Are we prisoners of our personal or collective history? A prison cell of belief can feel safe, but it is still a prison cell, and we are the only one who holds the key.

These are deep questions that we should consider as we look at each of the relationships in our lives and global conflicts.

You Are Going To Die

It is true, you are going to die. It may be today and it may not be for another eighty years, but it is something you can definitely count on.

I have done a fair bit of counseling in my time. I often sit with people who are in deep pain from major life challenges. But there are also occasionally those who come to me that are totally caught up in the minutiae of their daily dramas. It is almost as if they earned an academic degree in creating mountains out of molehills.

On those rare occasions I simply look them directly in the eye and say, "You know, you are going to die. I am going to die. Everyone that you know at this moment; all of your friends, all of your family, all of your colleagues and co-workers, everyone you read about in the newspaper – world leaders, celebrities, heroes – all of them will be dead within a hundred years." With that in mind, let's take another look at your issues.

Such a statement, while abrupt and shocking, brings us back to basics and helps us to put things in perspective. This sojourn on the Earth and all of our experience – whether pleasant or problematic – is quite temporary, just a brief moment in time. When we are tempted to get caught up in our daily dramas, it is helpful to pause and remember this, not as a cause for despair but to offer a perspective that allows us to laugh at ourselves and our inclination to suffer the deadly disease of "seriosity."

Bottom line, when you get really bogged down with your problems, put them in perspective and lighten up.

Mini-Me / Maxi-Me

It is a fact. We are multi-dimensional beings. We exist simultaneously in multiple dimensions. We are more than our bodies, our personalities, our egos, our possessions or even our beliefs. Those are just our 3D realities – a vehicle for our multi-dimensional self.

Why do I bring this up? It is because our perspective about life and the nature of reality shifts according to our dimensional level of perception. Most of the time all of us function from the 3D or what I like to call the 'mini-me' perspective. From this level of perception we experience our roller coaster of emotions such as anger, hatred, fear, desire, infatuation – and judgment. This isn't wrong or bad.

It's the nature of the human animal and our temporary embodiment in this dimension.

What most of us do not realize however is that we are much more than this. The authentic Self which exists at a higher frequency is the true occupant of that which we normally identify as "self."

This is what I call the maxi-me or what some refer to as the Higher Self. It is that part of us which sees the big picture – the macrocosm – and has a deeper understanding of our mini-dramas in life. It is that place within where the revered wisdom keepers, sages, gurus and holy folk of all ages have dwelt most of their time and which set them apart from their contemporaries.

A quick and easy way to reframe any situation or experience in your life is simply to shift your perspective from the mini-me default to your maxi-me. See it through a different set of eyes – a different mindset. Ask yourself "How would Divine Presence view this?" Use any appropriate term that serves you: God, Guardian Angel, or the Guru or avatar of your choice. Such an exercise can give you a fresh understanding of the situation and perhaps offer you a greater range of creative choices in how to deal with it.

Sex & Death
I grew up at a time and place where sex and death were not topics of polite conversation. In fact there seemed to be a silent conspiracy that these two topics were 'verboten.' And yet, both were the elephants in the room or the emperor with no clothes that no one dared to acknowledge, much less discuss. But that which isn't faced straightforward becomes a shadow that follows you throughout life with consequences that you may not anticipate nor desire. So what is it about sex & death?

If you are one of my great, great, great grandchildren, then by the time you read this I will have been 'dead' for many years. But trust me, it's no big thing.

We are constantly cycling in and out. Life itself is a process of change. As an adult you are no longer like you were as a child or teenager.

Though the essence may remain the same, the outer form is constantly evolving. Nothing is static. Death is simply another point of our ongoing growth and receives much more attention than it deserves. Of course you may lament the fact that people change, but your lamentations change nothing, so why waste your time?

The truth is, death, as it is normally perceived, is a grand lie – a deception – an illusion. It is a point of change in the ongoing cycle of life - yes. But the end all of existence? Definitely not.

We do live in a world of consequences and a world governed by frequencies and there are frequencies and consequences of our words and actions that can be utterly unpleasant or blissful but there isn't any physical heaven and hell except as you make it so. If you are really interested in knowing more about this, there are scores of books available that describe the journey between lives and what you can expect to experience. Or, if your current belief system satisfies you for the time being, stick to it.

Sex is the second 'biggie.' First and foremost it is a natural appetite, which is one of the components that come with the human vehicle you are traveling in this time around. Like the need for food, water & air, it is neither good nor bad. It simply serves a biological function to perpetuate the species. However we have - unlike all other species - attached a ton of baggage to sex. We have attached it to love, ownership, domination, religion and a host of other issues. Unlike breathing, however, which flows naturally and neutrally, we have made certain expressions of our sexuality good and bad, often with dire consequences.

OK, I agree. Sex isn't exactly like breathing. Because it involves reproduction, it can have long term consequences that any parent, and particularly single parents with full parental responsibility, can attest to. So yes, it is a biological function but it can also have consequences that an individual may or may not want. For this reason, it does involve some exceptional responsibility for those with reproductive capacity.

Sex can also be one of our most profound pieces of curriculum. When attached to the concept of love, it becomes much more than a biological function. In this case it becomes an emotional expression of the love which two people share or, in some cases, the love that one person holds for another. In addition to this, nature has created it with the same intensity as hunger, thirst or the need to breathe – with the added ingredient of intense pleasure. So without real love or the desire to procreate, it can be enjoyed for the pure pleasure of endorphin overload.

And then there is the concept of ownership so prevalent in traditional patriarchal societies. Women 'belong' to men and sex becomes an expression of that ownership, and often domination. In practice the man is free to have sex with whomever he will but – in some societies – such freedom can mean death for the woman.

Ownership in such societies also extends to the offspring. Family and linage are the household gods of such societies. How can you know that the children 'belong' to you if your wife isn't 'faithful?' And so sexual expression becomes an integral element in maintaining the patriarchal hierarchy.

So here we have four different meanings for sex
* Procreation
* An expression of love
* An expression of ownership and/or domination
* Pure pleasure

Is it any wonder that this has become such a rich piece of curriculum for the human experience? Any one of these alone could offer a lifetime of learning, but when you begin to mix them up and weave them together, it often results in a knotted tangle rather than a beautiful tapestry.

It is important to note here that, in spite of the prevalence of patriarchal societies that have prevailed into modern times, there are exceptions. Whereas an unmarried woman might be stoned to death in certain cultures for any expression of romantic love, in the traditional pre-missionary culture of certain islands of Polynesia, such as Tahiti, a woman was not deemed fit for marriage until she had give birth to her first child from her nocturnal frolics with the village lads. Why? Because the issue was fertility, not virginity. Until she proved that she was fertile she was not considered 'wife material.' And the children? They belonged to the village. Perhaps this is the origin of the saying "It takes a village to raise a child.'

Advice? The only advice I can offer is to be clear of your intent before allowing your hormones to dominate your experience. Are you seeking only pleasure? If so, be honest with yourself and others. Do not lead them to believe that it is an expression of authentic love. If you are primarily seeking love, do not fool yourself in to believing that every sexual experience will be just that.

There are those who give sex to get love and there are those who give love to get sex. Be clear before you start as to whether you want to bring children into the world with the lifetime of responsibilities this entails, and then handle things accordingly. Above all, go into any situation which you encounter with your eyes wide open. And whatever the results or consequences, remember that ultimately "Its all just curriculum."

On Being Gay

With eight grandchildren I assume it is safe to calculate that I may have more than 50 great, great, great grandchildren – for whom this is written. That being so, I also assume that it is safe to calculate that some of you may be attracted to those of your own gender. By the time you are born, it may well have been unequivocally proven by science that all of this is genetic, which I have always suspected. From bits and pieces of info I have gleaned about certain ancestors and distant cousins as well as personal experience, I suspect our family carries such a gene. To this end, I would offer some advice that your ancestors never had the benefit of.

First and foremost, don't let religion do a number on you. The superstitions of society have a very poor historical record in the area of human rights and these superstitions have more often than not been supported by organized religion, often with horrendous consequences. I'm a firm believer that "God don't make no junk."

Honor the way you were created, or the packaging that you chose for this lifetime. It is a gift and carries a certain kind of curriculum that can be invaluable to your soul growth.

Be aware that the dominant religions of Christianity Judaism and Islam grew out of very patriarchal tribal cultures. The great goddess had been dethroned and matriarchal religions had been conquered. It was believed that Man was made in the image of God and manhood was enshrined next to godliness.

During the patriarchal period, the ultimate archetype was the warrior. This was true, not only in the Middle east but throughout the world, including Europe, Asia and the Americas. Thus, anything that was perceived to threaten the concept of manhood or masculinity was up for destruction. This included the feminine principle and especially men who displayed anything feminine in either their demeanor or behavior. And this of course along with other traditional customs was supported and sanctified by the tribal religions.

While male homosexuality was condemned, very little was said about the love between women because this did not threaten the masculine principle. And more often than not, in a male relationship, it was only the submissive one who was considered 'wrong' – primarily due to the threat of the masculine ideal. Ultimately the issue wasn't religion or scriptures or any thing like this. The real issue was the assault on the primacy of masculine identity that served as the cornerstone of the patriarchal hierarchy. So keep this in mind.

Hopefully by the 22nd century this will no longer be an issue but if it is, understand it's real origin as the fragile and threatened masculine ego and not the word or will of God.

As we look at nature it seems to have a way of maintaining harmony. When something goes to an extreme and creates an imbalance, there seems to be an intelligence in nature that works to restore that balance. At this point in our history, the demands that an exploding human population have created on the natural resources of the Earth have produced a serious imbalance.

In the past when a species' population has outgrown its resources then nature has decreased such populations with starvation and disease and, in the case of humans, war. All of these have reduced the population but have also involved intense suffering.

I have no idea if there has been an actual increase in the 'gay' population or if it is just a major topic of conversation at this particular point in history. But if it is the former then is it possible that this is nature's more gentle way of decreasing the number of breeders on the planet? I don't know but it is an interesting idea to consider and it is certainly better way to reduce the population than disease, starvation and war.

It should also be noted that many indigenous cultures around the world held in high regard those who "walk between the worlds" of male and female. They were often the shamans and spiritual leaders of the tribe or village and served both as healers and mediators between the physical world and the world of Spirit. This was true in Africa, the Americas, Asia and Europe. If this is your natural state, consider it a gift and never let anyone shame or beat you up with their religious biases.

Chop Wood, Carry Water

The story is told of a novice monk asking his Zen Master what he did before he became enlightened. The master answered, "Chopped wood, carried water." He then asked, "Master, and what did you do after you became enlightened?" His answer? "Chopped wood, carried water."

This reminds me of one of my favorite sections of the Hua Hu Ching by the ancient Chinese sage, Lao Tzu, in which he says:

"Do you think you can clear your mind by sitting constantly in silent meditation? This makes your mind narrow, not clear."

'Integral awareness is fluid and adaptable, present in all places and at all times. That is true meditation.

'Who can attain clarity and simplicity by avoiding the world? The Tao is clear and simple, and it doesn't avoid the world.

'Why not simply honor your parents, love your children, help your brothers and sisters, be faithful to your friends, care for your mate with devotion, complete your work cooperatively and joyfully, assume responsibility for problems, practice virtue without first demanding it of others, understand the highest truths yet maintain an ordinary manner? That would be true clarity, true simplicity, true mastery."

It is the mundane aspects of life that provide us with the opportunities for soul growth; to experience and express love. On the spiritual journey often the unseasoned traveler is captivated by the scenery and loses sight of the destination.

I remember the abbot of a small Buddhist monastery of Cambodian monks telling me that on the journey to Nirvana there are many side paths. As one advances on the journey one will automatically become clairaudient, clairvoyant and clairsentient. One might even learn to levitate. However these are all sirens on the side of the road that can distract one from the destination.

So if one is addicted to conventional religion – whatever the brand – one may be captivated by and devoted to the ceremonies, rituals, dogma, scripture, organization, religious objects or the charisma of a leader. Or if one is on an alternative path, one may be just as devoted to mystical or esoteric notions and objects; crystals, chakras, ideas of ascension, extra terrestrials, ceremonies, etc.

However helpful these may be to one's personal journey, they are but tools and landmarks on the path but not the destination. To the extent that they become the sirens at the side of the road, distracting one from the final destination, they insure many additional lives before reaching the goal of returning to Source.

The quickest way to return Home isn't with all of the tools and toys, holy books and philosophies, ceremonies or fluff and flare of the spiritual world. It is to quietly work on ones own inner transformation – largely unseen by others – and to continue chopping wood and carrying water, especially if it is for the tired and weak who cannot chop their own wood and carry their own water.

So What's the Purpose of it All?

I have already addressed aspects of this in other sections such as "The Big Question" " Your Ultimate Objective" and "It's All Just Curriculum" in which I have indicated that our ultimate purpose on the planet is soul growth and all of our experiences are simply curriculum to that end. The pursuit of happiness, in whatever form that takes in our lives, is simply the carrot stick to move us forward. But beyond this, what is it all about. What is 'soul growth?"

For me it is the ongoing endeavor to increase or refine my frequency. At a soul level we are the in-breath and out-breath of Source. On the out-breath we move further and further away from Source until the pain of that separation initiates the souls desire to return and reunite with Source.

That vehicle is Love, pure and simple. Love is the highest frequency. It is the expressway for returning to Source. Increasing the frequency of love is the fastest path to Divine Presence. Jesus of Nazareth said it so well, living as he did in a time and with a religion complicated by hundreds of laws, customs and taboos. He said, "All of the laws and prophets are summed up in this one law, Love God with you heart, mind and soul and your neighbor as yourself."

In Buddhism the focus is on compassion, which is probably a better term than the much-maligned English term "love" which has so many different meanings and carries so much baggage.

For me it is simply the deep desire to want the very best for the other person or persons; for them to be happy, healthy, prosperous and free to pursue their highest and best. It is the basic teaching of most authentic historic spiritual teachers: Treat others the way you wish to be treated.

I recall one major turning point in my own life. It was a dream I had in 1985. While most dreams are visual, sometimes emotional and often jumbled, this was a clear voice that came to me saying, loud and clear "In the end you will be judged, not by the gods in whom you believe but by the quality of your love." It wasn't the quantity – how much I loved, but the quality – how well I loved: it was the frequency that was important.

This was particularly significant to me at that point in my life because I had been strongly influenced at that time by the Native American spiritual path, the focus of which was respect; respect for mother Earth and respect for "all my relations." I had noticed how people often treated others who they supposedly loved; how they said and did things they would not say or do if they truly respected the other person. This was particularly true within families, between spouses and between adults and children.

So when I had the big dream I had to rethink or reframe my understanding of love. I came to understand that respect and compassion were natural products of authentic love.

At this point in my life I understand that every experience is curriculum for my soul growth and what soul growth means is the ongoing endeavor to increase the frequency of love in my life and the bottom line is how I live my life day-to-day: What I think, what I say and how I treat others.

Have I arrived? I wish. I figure I will spend a few hundred more lifetimes working on this one. But at least I now know what the important thing is and I am consciously working on it.

Organized Religion

I remember my first visit to Thailand. I suppose that, prior to that visit, I had something of a romantic notion about Buddhism. Growing up immersed in a culture infected with fundamentalist Christianity and having read a bit of the teachings of Buddha, I admit to having had some of 'the grass is greener on the other side of the fence' notion which people often develop either out of curiosity or dissatisfaction.

However, when I saw Buddhism at ground zero in Thailand I found that it was no different than being Catholic in Rome, Jewish in Jerusalem, Muslim in the Mideast or Baptist in Georgia, USA. I found – as they say in Spanish "el mismo burro con otra montara." – the same donkey with a different saddle.

One of the things I came to realize is that human beings, for the most part, need religion, and organized religion – whatever the flavor – is about 95% cultural. I have noticed that people tend to take those customs, or issues, which were prevalent at the time and in the place where the religions founder lived and enshrined these as divine directives.

Most of the laws, rules and regulations are no more than human customs that were enshrined by the followers who organized a religion around the very basic teachings of the spiritual master. The Creator of the Universe could care less as to what you wear, what you eat or drink, where or with whom you sleep or the thousand and one other laws and rules you feel are necessary to appease God. While many of them may be useful, they, as well as the organized religions for which they serve as a foundation, are human creations.

Don't get me wrong. This doesn't make them bad. Organized religions, like governments and other human organizations, serve a purpose in society. They often provide vital social services, helping those who are having a hard time. They can provide a moral framework that serves as glue in holding society together and providing a guide star for socially approved behavior or even serving a prophetic role with governments. Organized religion may even provide a garden-variety kind of spiritual guidance and leadership for the masses who might otherwise have no interest in things beyond food, shelter and material security. So it has its purpose.

The down side, however, is when it is used – as it often is – to suppress freedom of thought and behavior simply because they go against cultural tradition. I think of those religious sects who 'shun' members who leave the fold and refuse to sit at the same table or even speak to those who have left. Or consider those who – in the name of religion or morality – would kill their own daughter, niece or other female family member because they 'dishonored' the family and religion by kissing a boy.

There is nothing spiritual in this, it is all about control, and the keepers of organized religion do not have a good history when it comes to exercising their power of control over the masses. Too often they have shared the same bed with oppressive governments and sanctioned unspeakable horrors in the name of God.

But we shouldn't throw the baby out with the wash, nor should we condemn all for the behavior of a few. As people are different, so are the organizations they create. Do not believe what the various spiritual teachers or religious leaders tell you. Look at their lives and the products of their religions. As the wise saying goes "judge the tree by its fruit."

All of this brings me again to some of my favorite quotations from the Tao Te Ching, written by Lao Tsu who lived 2,500 years ago in ancient China: *"Do not go about worshipping deities and religious institutions as the source of subtle truth. To do so is to place intermediaries between yourself and the Divine, and makes yourself a beggar who looks outside for a treasure that is hidden in his own heart." (#17) Or again...*

"Dualistic thinking is a sickness. Religion is a distortion. Materialism is cruel. Blind spirituality is unreal. Chanting is no more holy than listening to the murmur of a stream. Counting prayer beads no more holy than simply breathing. Religious robes no more spiritual than work clothes. If you wish to attain oneness with the Tao don't get caught up in spiritual superficialities. Instead, live a quiet and simple life, free of ideas and concepts.

'Find contentment in the practice of undiscriminating virtue, the only true power. Giving to others selflessly and anonymously, radiating light throughout the world and illuminating your own darkness, your virtue becomes a sanctuary for yourself and all beings." (#75) And last of all...

"There are many partial religions and then there is the Integral Way. Partial religions are desperate, clever human inventions. The Integral Way is a deep expression of the pure, whole universal mind. Partial religions rely on the hypnotic manipulation of undeveloped minds. The Integral Way is founded on the free transmission of the plain, natural immutable truth; it is a total reality, not an occult practice.

The integral way eschews conceptual fanaticism, extravagant living, fancy food, and violent music. They spoil the serenity of one's mind and obstruct one's spiritual development. Renouncing what is fashionable and embracing what is plain, honest and virtuous, the integral Way returns you to the subtle essence of life. Adopt its practices and you will become like they are: honest, simple, true, virtuous, whole.

You see, in partial pursuits, one's transformation is always partial as well. But in integral self-cultivation, it is possible to achieve a complete metamorphosis, to transcend your emotional and biological limitations and evolve to a higher state of being." (#78)

As you can see, there are very few ideas in the world that are new. When I have been asked in the past when I was going to write a book, I have always answered 'probably never, because I have nothing new to share that hasn't already been said by those who are far beyond me in their literary abilities and thinking.' This is the reason this is addressed to my descendants. It is simply a gift to you that I would have liked to have received from my own ancestors; wondering who they were and how they thought. If my perspective is also helpful in your journey, that's great. If not, then perhaps it may at least be entertaining.

Bottom line? Avail yourself to many perspectives, both spiritual, political, scientific and otherwise and then use your left brain logic and your right brain intuition to decide what makes the most sense to you and what works the best for you at this moment in your life. But don't let any individual or any organization, whether religious or political, think for you. Religious and political tyrants thrive on the shoulders of unthinking, uncritical followers.

Falling in love
Ah yes! Another 'biggie.' This is something that you will likely have to deal with at least once, and perhaps many times in life. It's natures' design (trick?) to keep the species going and much of it is based on myth: Fall in love, get married and live happily ever after. Oh, if it were only true! But simple observation seems to indicate otherwise.

Why is this so? It is because the very foundation of the myth is a lie. We never fall in love with another person. We fall in love with the fantasy of what we want that person to be for us. The truth is, what we call 'love' is in fact infatuation; an intense passionate attraction to another person that blinds us to everything about that person except their highest and best, whether real or imagined.

However, as time passes and with some experience together, the veil of infatuation which clouds the eyes begins to fade and you begin to see a real person and not a fantasy. This is commonly referred to as "the honeymoon is over."

But infatuation plays an important role in the human condition so I'm not condemning it. I'm only shinning a little light on it so that we can really see what it is and what it isn't. First of all, it plays an important biological role in holding two peoples attention long enough for them to - perhaps — learn to love each other and/or potentially propagate the species.

Authentic love is a learning process and something that can only be learned once the fantasy has faded and reality has set in. It is only when you see the real person, with all of their imperfections, that you can begin to love them. Until that time you are simply infatuated with the fantasy you have of them. This is the basis of the term "love is blind."

It's also the basis of the common phenomena of "The honeymoon is over." It means the two people have woken up to the reality of who each is and what they do and don't have together. Infatuation is emotional based and temporary while authentic love includes an emotional element but involves much, much more, and is grounded in commitment. It's going to be around even when the going gets rough - as it inevitably will.

Unfortunately - because we have been lied to as to the nature of love - when the infatuation fades, we believe that we have "fallen out of love" and too often go in search of a new "high" that infatuation brings. Infatuation is oh so delicious! It is also very deceiving if one isn't clear.

Don't get me wrong. I'm not opposed to 'falling in love' or infatuation. It is one of the grandest feelings in the world and I 'love' it!!! But at my age, I see it for what it is and isn't, and don't take myself too seriously.

One of the things I have noticed in myself is that when I 'fall in love' I get totally stupid, so one of the commitments I have made to myself is not to make any big decisions while I am 'under the influence.' I've made some pretty stupid 'mistakes' in the past while under the influence of cupid's spell. Or we could say that I've attracted some very challenging 'curriculum.'

When the infatuation fades - as it ultimately will - you have the opportunity to really learn to love the person you are with - in all of their imperfections. No, they will not fulfill all of your hopes, desires or fantasies. They aren't on the planet to make your dreams come true. And yes, they fart in bed sometimes.

It's when you come to this reality that you have the opportunity to learn to love in spite of it all. Learning to love is like learning anything else. It has its curriculum and it is work and sometimes it's hard.

To the extent that you pin your happiness on what another person does or does not do - to the extent that they fulfill or fail to fulfill your needs - to that extent you and your happiness are their prisoner and you are the only one who has the key.

So let us enjoy the infatuation 'micro-chip' that Mother Nature gave us. But let us not confuse it with authentic love

The Preposition Oracle

As human beings we are fond of oracles. We like to know what the future holds. It gives us some sense of control or at least an opportunity to prepare for what may come. I am quite familiar with the many varieties of oracles and there is some validity to this.

What was once seen as mere superstition can now be better understood through the science of quantum mechanics. Oracles are much like a weather report; basing predictions on patterns not readily observable to the average person. But with all of this, I have found the most reliable oracle for predicting your future is the prepositions you use in interpreting things that happen to you. Let me explain.

When something unpleasant happens, do you say or think "Why did this happen *To* me?" Or do you say or think "Why did this happen *For* me?" Which of these two simple prepositions you use is a reflection of the way you view the world.

You are either living in a world in which you are a victim of circumstances and other people's actions or you are living in a world in which you attract circumstances or events that are rich curriculum for soul growth.

The first is a reflection of victim mentality and your happiness is held hostage to what someone else does or does not do. In the second case, every one – and especially those who push your buttons – are your most valuable gurus – God in Drag, if you will.

So you can largely predict your own future by looking at which of these two prepositions serve as the foundation of your thinking. Victim mentality will take you one direction in life that will seldom be a pleasant journey or lead to a happy ending.

On the other hand, seeing every person and situation in your life – however unpleasant – as curriculum that you have attracted at some level for your own soul growth will empower you to become a conscious creator of what you do want rather than a complainer about what you don't want.

We learn by contrast. As you have heard, the mountain is only as high as the valley is low. Intense desire for something is often the result of experiencing it's opposite. Unpleasant events, circumstances or individuals help us to get very clear as to what we don't want in our lives, and this clarity helps us to pivot into seeing what we really do want. So those unpleasant experiences – while undeniably uncomfortable – serve a vital purpose in our growth. So instead of playing the victim, blaming others and whining "why me," find the blessing, the hidden gift. Ask you self why this happened FOR you.

In Every Seeming Adversity

I recall listening to the lecture of a motivational speaker who began his lecture by saying that nothing bad ever happened to him after he turned 40 years old. Since he was obviously at least 60, this caused everyone in the room to sit up and pay attention. "What was his secret?" was the thought that was on everyone's mind.

He went on to say that of course, many unpleasant things had occurred over the course of years, as they do in each of our lives. But each time they did, he said "this is good" and each time he was able to find something of benefit in the event or circumstance. It was simply a mental habit he had developed which automatically directed his mind in finding the gift in every situation, however unpleasant.

It reminds me of a statement that I read many years ago that has become a guide star in my own life. "In every seeming adversity is the seed of an equal or greater benefit." Note the word seed. It may only be a very tiny seed and once found that seed may need to be carefully nurtured if it is to produce fruit.

But too often we are so occupied with the unpleasant smell of the manure of circumstance and we can't find or don't even think to look for that seed of value. We see the mature as so much crap in our lives instead of realizing that it may be rich fertilizer for our soul growth.

You have heard the saying "time will tell." I have often found in my own life that events that were incredibly unpleasant at the time of occurrence –viewed from a distance - ended up being some of the richest blessings in my life. When unpleasant things happen, we are prone to 'premature evaluation' or snap judgments as to what is good or bad. While there is no denying that something is pleasant or unpleasant, there is wisdom in reserving judgment as to the good and bad of it. Only time will be able to render final judgment. This reminds me a favorite Chinese folk tale.

A Chinese Folk Tale
There is a story of a poor farmer with a son who was his pride and joy and a

white stallion horse that was his most prized possession. One day his white horse ran away and the villagers came to him and said, "You are such an unlucky man. It is so bad." The farmer answered, "Maybe it's bad, maybe it's good."

The next day the stallion returned with twelve wild horses following him. The same villagers returned to tell the farmer how lucky he was. The farmer answered, "Maybe it's good, maybe it's bad."

The next day, his son broke his leg while attempting to train one of the wild horses. And the villagers said, "This is terrible! You are so unlucky." The farmer said, "Maybe its bad, maybe it's good."

Three days later the Army came to the village and conscripted all the young men in the village except the farmer's son, because had a broken leg. Once more the villagers went on about his good fortune. They said, "You are so lucky not to have your son go off to war." The farmer replied, "Maybe it's good, maybe it's bad."

This is a good example of the villagers suffering from premature evaluation.

It Just Do What It Do
It is said that the cornerstone teaching of the Buddha is that 'desire is the source of all suffering.' And yet, we has humans are born with desire; the desire to eat, sleep, reproduce and have freedom and security. On these we build a thousand other desires. When these desires are frustrated, then he is correct. It is the source of suffering.

Desires give birth to goals and the pursuit of goals give purpose to life, even when those desires and goals are spiritual, such as 'enlightenment.' So I will not negate desire or goals. It is a part of the equipment we were given when we incarnated for a human experience. I will agree, however that attachment is the source of all suffering.

I am fond of saying that there is only one source to all relationship problems and that is "you jus don't do what you suppose to do." In other words, your suffering in a relationship is the result of the other person not doing or being what you expect – or attached to. When you accept things as they are and not as you wish, then your suffering dissolves. So let's examine this more closely.

Being a farmer teaches me just about all I need to know about life and spirit. First and foremost I know that, to be successful, I must work in cooperation with nature and natural cycles. Secondly I know that I must have desire, goals and intentions. I must have the desire to plant certain crops and give the attention necessary to all of the activities involved in caring for them. However, once planted and nurtured, I must surrender to nature. If I become attached to a certain outcome – so many bushels per crop or acre, I am setting myself up for potential disappointment; i.e. suffering.

Desire, goals, intentions and even expectations are not the source of suffering. It is only when you become attached to an outcome that you set yourself up for suffering. The individual, event or circumstance is not the source of your suffering. It is your attachment to the person, event or circumstance being different than what they really are.

So how is this accomplished? Letting go of judgment is a good start. The way I see it, there are three ways of looking at everything: "That's good, that's bad and that's interesting." The older I get the more my judgments fade and everything simply becomes 'interesting.'

One of my favorite sayings – straight from the hood – is "it jus do what it do." This is very Zen. It shows both an acknowledgment and an acceptance of the isness of things. It simply is what it is. While I receive a reasonably good score in the isness test in my personal life, I will admit to challenges in taking this approach when it involves social or political issues which are the basis of massive human suffering. In this area I am still a work in progress and have much yet to do.

One of my inspirations is the story of the Zen Monk who lived in a mountain hermitage on the coast of Japan. There was a village some few miles distance and one day a young lass of the village found herself pregnant by one of the young fishermen she had been secretly seeing. When the baby was born, the village elders demanded to know who the father was.

Not wanting to implicate her secret lover she told them that the hermit monk on the mountain was the father. The village elders took the baby and with the whole village marched to the mountain hermitage and banged on the door. When the old monk appeared they thrust the baby into his arms and said 'here, this is yours, you take care of it,' to which he replied 'Ahso' (it is what it is).

Several years later, the young woman and the fisherman were married and after their first child, they began to feel regret for having blamed their first child on the hermit monk. So, swallowing their pride they went to the village elders and confessed. Thereupon the village elders, followed by all of the villagers, marched again to the mountain hermitage and banged on the door. When the old monk opened the door, standing next to him was a six-year-old lad dressed in the robes of a novice monk. The village elders apologized profusely for having blamed the old monk and having left the child with him. They then took the child, without further discourse, and started back to the village. The old monk, standing alone in the doorway, simply said "Ahso."

He had reached a level of mastery that I may never know for many life times, if at all. But whether authentic or apocryphal, the story offers the ultimate illustration of surrendering to the 'it just do what it do.'

The Dog Track Theory of Life

A few years ago I developed what I call the Dog Track theory of life. At the time I was having an in depth discussion with a friend who was devoted to a certain teacher who insisted that our primary purpose for being on the Earth was to experience joy.

While I loved the idea, I did not find it consistent with either my personal experience or what I had learned from working with clients in hypnosis. As I thought about this and the powerful appeal of such an idea I came to realize a few things.

The pursuit happiness (joy) is the most fundamental motivator in human existence. The form that takes is as varied as are humans themselves. Beyond the basics of food, shelter, clothing, security and freedom, we have a thousand different things that we believe will make us happy.

Unlike my friend, I believe our purpose on the planet is soul growth and we attract or create those circumstances that serve as curriculum to this end. All of the things we desire in our pursuit of happiness are simply carrot sticks that propel us forward.

This is how I came about developing what I call the dog track theory of life. Now I must admit that I have never attended a dog race but I am familiar with the process. The dogs are in their little stalls, the spectators are in the stadium bleachers, and there is a metal rabbit that keeps running just ahead of the dogs as they pursue it around the track. The gun goes off, the gates go up and the dogs are off and running.

The metal rabbit is the 'pursuit of happiness' in whatever form this may take in an individual's life. Each of us has those goals or desires that we feel will make us happy once they are reached. However, if we are honest with ourselves, we will have to admit that in the past, each time we met one of our goals or fulfilled one of our desires it gave us only a momentary sense of satisfaction and then we were off in pursuit of the next goal or desire. None of them really brought us lasting happiness.

For this reason I contend that the real purpose of the metal rabbits in our lives are really for inspiring us to action which results in experience. It is the experience that provides the curriculum for our soul growth. Therefore the pursuit of happiness is the metal rabbit that cause us to have those experiences that contribute to our growth and this human experience is indeed a school.

What If....

As I have already indicated in several other sections, I hold to the idea that we are not victims of circumstance. Rather all of the events and circumstances of our lives we have attracted at some level for our growth.

Objectively speaking this may or may not be true and you may or may not believe it, but if you do embrace this idea it definitely changes the way you see the world and more importantly it empowers you in a way that few things can. As the saying goes, change you mind and your world changes. Easier said than done, right?

Here is an interesting exercise for those with a good imagination. The next time someone pushes your buttons or says or does something which causes you to react defensively and/or feel victimized, simply pretend that it is all just a grand drama with you as the lead actor. Not only are you playing the lead role, but you are also the script writer and director who has hired all of the others to play a part in your drama. The whole purpose of the drama is to awaken you to who you really are.

With this perspective, look again at each of the actors, especially those who are playing an adversarial or protagonist role in your drama. Why did you hire them as actors in your drama? Instead of blame can you honor their perfect performance and come to understand why you have created this drama and what it is teaching you about yourself and the world?

Keep in mind that you are pretending for the creative purpose of reframing or looking at the situation from another perspective; a perspective that will empower you rather than keep you locked in the victim mentality founded on blame for what someone else did or didn't say or do.

What has been said or done has been said or done. At this point it just is and there is little you can do to change the situation. However, how you decide to view it is totally within your own power. It can become either a stumbling stone or a building block for creating the kind of future you want.

So the next time something occurs, instead of taking a knee jerk reaction to attack or complain, expand your freedom of possibilities and ask yourself "What if I really attracted this in to my life? Why would I have done that? What purpose could it serve me?" If you pause long enough to sit quietly with this question, you may be surprised with the answer you receive.

As Within, So Without
There was a time, when I was in my 20's, that I thought my mission was to save the world. It was the 1960's and I was not alone. We took it upon ourselves to fight injustice, resist war and right the wrongs of the world.

Looking back now I don't regret a moment of my own activism but I do see how arrogant I was and honestly, how stupid as well. At that time I thought you changed the world by changing the outer circumstances.

However as I learned more and more history, I began to notice a pattern. It seemed that the idealistic young people throughout history, who brought down tyrants in the name of freedom and justice, more often than not, themselves became dictators who committed atrocities as bad or worse than the ones they replaced. Why was this so?

I also had the fortune to visit the land of Jerusalem several times and work with close friends – both Jewish and Palestinian – who were involved in peace work. Very often I saw dedicated individuals come up with dozens of good plans for peace in the region but nothing ever came of it. Why was this so?

These and similar experiences helped me to finally realize that the only authentic and lasting revolution was a revolution in consciousness. All of the horrors of human behavior were fundamentally the reflection of the consciousness of the people. You could have a revolution and change outer circumstances but until there was a transformation of consciousness, there would be no fundamental change in society – only a temporary superficial veneer; the old donkey with a different saddle.

That marked a shift in the direction of my life from fighting 'the system' to working to undermine the kind of consciousness that made the system viable. I started understanding the meaning of "as within, so without."

And then I took it one step further. While I might continue to be involved in external efforts to improve the world or provide transformational opportunities for others, my first and foremost responsibility was to work on me – not to fix you.

All of the wisdom teachers I have studied and respected concur that planetary transformation begins with personal transformation. When you change, your world changes. So instead of feeling a personal responsibility for changing others, I first assume responsibility for my own transformation.

This also goes along with the idea of 'walking your talk' or 'your actions speak so loud, I can't hear what you are teaching or preaching.' So sometimes the greatest teaching we can offer the world is simply modeling in our own behavior the kind of world we envision. In such a case it isn't even necessary to open our mouth.

The Three Approaches To Problems

Each of us – over the course of our lives – have to deal with problems. How successful we are in dealing with them is largely dependant on our approach. For example, I am nearing 70 yeas old and I haven't had any problems for at least 30 years. OK, I have had more than a few challenges, many of which have been very unpleasant but I made the decision 30 years ago that I would start seeing these situations as challenges rather than problems. That change of attitude brought a whole new set of resources to the forefront in dealing with situations.

Whether we consider them problems or challenges, the first thing we normally do with such situations is try to find a way to fix or solve the problem. If something is broken, you fix it. If you have a problem, your first response is to solve it. Many such challenges can be solved or fixed, but there are those that have no solutions. If a loved one is killed in an accident, you can't fix it.

So the next approach is trying to understand the 'why' of it. This is where the concept of 'life curriculum' comes in. If we can look at any event or situation in our life as curriculum for soul growth, it takes on a new meaning. The pain may remain but if we are courageous enough to delve deep into the situation, we may learn valuable things about our world and ourselves.

We may not be able to fix the problem and we may not even be able to understand and give it meaning for our lives, but there is one final question: "How can we use it."

History and personal biographies are full of stories of crisis in people's lives that were tragically painful and yet transformative. The insurmountable problem marked a turning point in their life that took them from breakdown to breakthrough.

It is the old story of taking the lemons that life gives us and making lemonade or using the stones in our path as building blocks instead of stumbling stones. Is it easy? No way. But it seems the difficulty of the challenge is the very foundation of the transformation.

Now these three approaches; solving, finding meaning, using a problem, are not mutually exclusive. In fact, they can go hand in hand.

However, we seldom go on to number two and three if we can easily solve the problem to begin with. We usually only seek meaning or find a way to use the situation for those problems we cannot solve.

Life's challenges provide a rich training ground for using all three approaches as a part of our soul growth curriculum.

What is Wisdom?

One of the things I have noticed, both from my university studies and subsequent experience in life, is that intelligence has very little to do with wisdom. Intelligence has been defined as "the ability to learn or understand or to deal with new or trying situations; the ability to apply knowledge to manipulate one's environment or to think abstractly as measured by objective criteria." In such high esteem is intelligence held, that we have developed tests to determine and score the intelligence level of an individual. Universities and science particularly are full of some of the most intelligent people on the planet.

But one thing puzzles me. Why is it that some of the greatest atrocities of the 20th century were committed by some of the most highly educated and supposedly intelligent people? Consider for example Germany, the United Kingdom, the USA and Japan?

I would contend that intelligence has very little to do with wisdom. Wisdom is defined as knowledge gained from experience, whether one's own experience or that of others. It is, from a Native American perspective, an understanding of the effects of our words or actions on the planet or others for seven generations.

36

Intelligence is important and valuable, but when it is sterile, without the wisdom of the heart and experience, it can lead to disaster, as we have seen in our recent history.

The greatest gift you can give to your children is to teach them wisdom. Teach them to consider the potential long-term effects of their words or actions.

I remember clearly offering guidance to a young couple who were at war with one another at the end of a bitter divorce. They were totally possessed by emotion and ego. They were saying things to one another, and often in front of the children, that I could see was creating long-term damage and leaving scars that might never heal. These were two intelligent people but were totally blinded by anger and ego.

If they had even an ounce of wisdom and were willing to consider the long-term effect of what they were saying and doing, then they would have resisted the temptation to emotional knee jerk reactions. Rather they would look at what they wanted to accomplish and the actions needed to reach their goal. As it was, they were in a state of possession, and continued on a path of self-sabotage which injured not only themselves but their family as well.

The greatest gift you can offer your children is the understanding of the implications of their actions. Not that they will be punished for doing or saying certain things but rather the potential harm that their words and actions can cause both to themselves and others. It is known as the law of return or "what goes around, comes around." Some will understand that the stove is hot and they shouldn't touch it. Others, unfortunately, must learn from the experience of being burned. Wisdom is the understanding that 'this leads to that.' Do not expect to treat others badly without being treated badly in return. That, unfortunately, is human nature.

Two Roads
Relationships are one of the biggest challenges that most people face at some point in their life. Sometimes with parents, sometimes with children, sometimes with other family members, coworkers, employers; the list is endless.

So often we respond to these challenges in a 'knee jerk' kind of way born of ego and based on emotion without really thinking through our desired outcome. But the truth is, we always have a choice in the way we react and the choice we make will determine the outcome we experience.

In dealing with personal challenges, and especially relationships, I call these two options the high road and the low road. I do not speak symbolically here but literally; the road with the lowest frequency, guided by ego and the road of the highest frequency, guided by Spirit.

Each road leads to a different destination. It's not really a matter of good and bad or right and wrong. It's not even about the other person. It's a matter of being very clear about my desired destination in life and choosing the road that will take me there. The basic question is "Where do I want to end up?" Once I have decided that, I can choose the road that will take me there.

If I don't consciously choose my destination, then my initial knee-jerk reaction is to take the first road, the road of ego. This is the broad and easy road and it's the only road that most people know. If I choose to take this road then I would be very offended at what the other person did and said. My first response would be to retaliate with hurt for hurt. I would see myself as a victim and the other person being totally at fault. I would have a need to be right and the other person to be wrong. I would talk to all my friends and try to get them to be on my side just to prove to myself that I am right and the other person is wrong. I would need to win and have the other person lose. I would need to feel superior and the other person inferior. I would need to dictate what the other person should do or be according to my own ideas. I would get a certain satisfaction in revenge -- wanting the other person to feel the hurt that I feel.

The signposts on this road are anger, hatred, mistrust, dishonesty, disrespect & fear. It is a low road because it carries a very low frequency. It is the road of war, constant battle and never ending conflict. I have taken this road before, and even when I have "won" a battle, it didn't bring me peace, joy or true satisfaction. It left me empty because ultimately it was a dead end. The irony is that I never chose this road consciously because I never really consciously chose the destination I wanted to reach.

The second road is much narrower and not so easy. It is the high road and carries the higher frequency of Spirit. If I choose this road then I will see the other person as a parent who sees a child who is throwing a tantrum - a child who is in deep pain, feeling rejected, bewildered, scared and hurt. I would also see through all of the ego drama into the heart and essence of a beautiful soul who has not discovered it's own beauty. If I took the high road I would assume personal responsibility for co-creating the existing situation - not blaming the other person or myself - but realizing that we both created the situation by the choices we made. If I took the high road I would not allow the other person's choices to pull me down to the low road, because I would be the master of my own journey.

I would act rather than react. I would have responsibility for nothing but managing my own frequency and my own journey. I would have no need to win but only to find win/win solutions to common challenges. The signposts on this road are compassion, kindness, generosity, cooperation, respect, trust, honesty and love. And these are also its destination. The few times I have stepped out of my ego pain and taken this road, it has led to bliss.

How all of this would play out in a specific situation, I can't predict. It would depend on the individuals involved and the situation. Would I take the high road or the low road now if I were under attack? That I can't really predict either. In one sense, the road one takes isn't really a conscious choice as much as an automatic response according to one's own frequency. As Jesus said "You will know a tree by its fruit." We each respond according to our own frequency level.

This is why I spend a good deal of time in silence. For me, silence is a good time to work on my own frequency. As much as I might want peace in the world, I have come to realize that I cannot create that for anyone but myself. I can't solve anyone else's problems, take away their hurt or make them different from what they are. I can only work on myself and hold the intention of love and blessings and know - or at least hope - that at some level, it all is in Divine Order.

Predicting the Future

Cultures throughout the world and throughout history have had systems of divination for predicting the future. While science scoffs at such stuff and delegates it to the realm of superstition, there is no less interest in it today than there was in ancient times. Why is this so? Is it only a reflection of the human desire to control one's future, or has it endured because people have found it helpful? And if there are those people or those systems that can predict the future, then what does this say about free will? I have heard it said from many sources that the Earth is a planet of free will. If this is so, then how can the future already be known?

I have wrestled with this problem for some time since I hold both positions as valid. I do believe in free will and the ability to choose our future. At the same time I know it is possible for some people and systems to accurately predict the future. Here is how I have reconciled these two ideas at this point in my life. As the ancient mystics have taught, outside of this dimension there is no time; no past, no future, just NOW. While this idea feels right, I will admit that I am too dense to wrap my mind around it.

I do find it interesting however that experiments in quantum physics are now suggesting the same thing; that at the quantum level there isn't past and future, or 'this before that'. Rather, it appears that it's all in the present.

What is much more understandable to me is the concept of reading patterns. The best example of this is a weather report. The weather reporter tells us that rain, snow or sunshine is predicted and normally gives a percentage of possibilities of this occurring, based on reading and understanding weather patterns. Of course we know that these predictions don't always come true but they are valid enough that a whole television station is devoted to just weather prediction.

So how does this relate to predicting human behavior? Again, it is based on patterns. While we do have free will, we are very predictable and easily influenced. In fact, the whole multi-billion dollar advertising industry is built on the fact of how easily we can be influenced and how predictable we are as habitual creatures.

In addition to this, when we choose to incarnate on planet Earth, part of the agreement involved accepting a certain set of rules that govern this dimension. For example, even though we have free will, we cannot stand outside, flap our arms up and down and expect to fly.

It doesn't work that way. There are certain 'natural laws' that govern this dimension. And we chose some 'packaging' in terms of bodies, family, personality type and such things as astrological and numerological aspects determined by our time of birth – all of which give us a frame of reference which can either limit or enhance our free will, depending on how conscious we are of the influences.

But the greatest inhibitor of free will is our belief system. We are all prisoners of our beliefs. We cannot do or go beyond the limits of our beliefs about ourselves or our world.

The Warehouse of Possibilities
In the study of history it is always interesting to see the issues that dominated a particular era and culture, and I wonder what it will be for you in the 22nd

Century. Obviously any period of history features many areas of interest. The things that I speak of as current concerns may be totally foreign to some of my contemporaries whose lives are built around other interests such as sports, and they may be amusing to you, my descendants.

But I have always been the explorer, venturing to the edge of the known world of human consciousness, so I admit that the subjects I speak of are not prime topics of the mainstream. Let me reflect on a couple of these.

There is a significant contingent of the US population – thanks to the internet - that is devoted to the notion that we live in a world controlled by conspiracies fostered by a variety of secret entities such as "the shadow government" the "global elite" or the "illuminati."

I have delved deep into these matters because I feel that it is important to be well informed, whether or not one chooses to embrace a particular belief system. In the case of conspiracies, I do not reject the validity of many of these claims, nor do I embrace all of them. I simply pay attention.

What I have learned is this. As mentioned in a previous section, we all wear a set of glasses based on our belief system and it is through these glasses that we view the world. None of us truly see the world objectively. It is always seen through the eyes of our belief systems, whether religious, political, social, cultural, etc.

If you believe in monsters, you will find one in every closet. The same is true with angels. A glass is either half full or half empty, depending on how you see the world.

Most of us are familiar with the phenomena of purchasing a car and then suddenly starting to notice all of the other cars on the road of the same model and color that you never noticed before. They were there all along but you did not see them because your attention was focused elsewhere, until you bought one yourself.

We all live in a warehouse of possibilities. Let me explain. Imagine if you will that you are standing in the middle of a huge warehouse. It is pitch dark and you have a flashlight with a powerful beam. Every possible experience in your life is lined up along the wall of this warehouse. In one corner there are monsters that are just waiting to attack you. In another corner is a stack of gold, gems and jewels representing unbelievable and unlimited prosperity. In

another corner sits the most exquisite romantic relationship you can imagine....
Just waiting.

The list is endless. Everything you could possibly imagine – both pleasant and unpleasant - exists in this warehouse as a potential. What you experience, however, is determined by where you point your flashlight – or focus your attention. The moment you focus your steady attention on any of these possibilities, they wake up and become an active part of your experience.

So the question is, if you really want to experience good health, why are you always talking about your health problems? If you want to have a good relationship with a person, why are you always telling them, yourself and others about all of their faults? If you want to be prosperous why are you always acting and talking like a poor person? Or why do you continually reinforce the idea of victimhood by focusing on "them" and what "they" are doing?

Have you ever noticed the popular game that people play called "ain't it awful." Here is how it works. One person will mention something that "they" are doing or talk about one of their personal problems and before you know it everyone is in on the game, giving examples of how awful it is and soon the whole group has spiraled downward in to a pit of despair and defeat. It seems that they getting some morbid satisfaction in sharing gloom.

Now that is fine if you are more interested in playing the game rather than improving the situation. But I will be honest, I have seen a lot of people playing the 'ain't it awful' game but I have never seen a group of people sitting around informally and getting high just discussing how great things are or exploring creative solutions to the worlds challenges.

If we put a fraction of the energy we invest in complaining about 'them' – into really working on implementing solutions, how different the world would be. It all goes back to the old saying; it's better to like a candle, however small, than to curse the darkness. So pay attention to what or where you are shinning your light or focusing your attention, because you can be sure that's what you will be experiencing.

Additional Writings
The foregoing was written during the winter of 2014 and reflects my thinking at that time. As I am fond of telling friends, "do not hold me to this next Tuesday." Why? Because I may experience or learn something that will expand my

thinking on some of these areas of interest. What follows are some additional things I have written over the past 15 years. I include them as a way of offering additional insight as to who I am at the idea level.

The Galactic Fairytale (May 2000)

A long, long time ago in a galaxy far, far away there were all of these little light beings just hanging out enjoying life in that joyful & timeless dimension. And then one day a very large, magnificent angel came to them. He had a very serious look on his face. He was looking for volunteers for a very important cosmic mission.

"We have this small, but very special planet out at the edge of the galaxy called Gaia. It is quite unique, like a beautiful garden and it is teeming with hundreds of thousands of different life forms. It has been something of an experimental station in the galaxy and it has a most interesting humanoid life form that incorporates the very highest and lowest frequencies known in the cosmos. It is in fact the very epitome of dualism. On the one hand it is an incredibly beautiful life form and is capable of carrying the highest frequencies of love, light & joy known throughout the whole Universe. On the other hand it is capable of carrying the densest and darkest frequencies the cosmos has ever experienced - frequencies that the rest of creation evolved beyond eons ago.

Here is the current situation. Within the domain of time, this planet goes through periodic cosmic cycles. It is now coming to the end of two major cycles - a 2,000 year long age of Pisces and the 25,000 year long cosmic year in its journey around the central sun of the milky way galaxy.

With the completion of this cycle, many things are coming to an end and many things are about to begin. But most importantly, the planet is experiencing an infusion of light that is dramatically increasing its frequency. As during any major time of transition, there will be a certain amount of turbulence. Some of this will be geological, for Gaia herself is a living planet and is also evolving. But much of it also involves the hominoid species that dominates the planet.
This will not be a particularly easy time for the species - especially for those who are sleeping and those who are vibrating at the lowest frequencies. As the frequency changes it will create insecurity that in turn will create fear.

The first era of evolution on this planet was the physical era and the key word was survival. The second era, which is now ending, was the mental era and the key word was logic. The third era, which is now beginning, is the era of the heart and the key word is love. This is the highest frequency.

Those who currently hold the reign of power on the planet are of the old order of the physical & mental. To the extent that they can make a graceful transition to a heart centered and divinely guided life, it will be an easy transition. To the extent that they are unable to do this, they will experience much turmoil.

So this is the current situation of Gaia. The reason I am here is to seek volunteers who would be willing to incarnate in humanoid form on the planet at this time to help make this an easy and smooth transition. We have sent prophets and teachers in the past. Very often they were brutally persecuted or killed. In other instances they were set up as "gods" to be worshiped and these humanoids built elaborate religions and rituals around them and used these religions to control each other. They did everything except follow the simple teachings that were offered.

So this time we are trying a different approach. No more prophets, saviors & avatars that they can use to create religions. This time we are sending in thousands - actually hundreds of thousands - of ordinary light beings with only two assignments:

1) Stay in your heart. Regardless of what happens, stay in your heart.
2) Remember who you are, why you are here and what this is all about.

Now that seems easy enough, right? Unfortunately, No! As I have said, duality has reached its peak on this planet. This species has perfected the illusion of good and evil. The greatest challenge you will experience is to remember Who You Really Are, Why You Are Here and What This Is Really All About. When you remember, you will be able to stay in your heart, regardless of external events.

So how will you know when you are forgetting? It is easy. Watch your judgments. The moment you notice that you are in a place of judgment you will know that you have forgotten Who You Really Are, Why You Are Here and What This Is Really All About. That will be your signal.

Now here is the challenge. Life on this planet will require a great deal of discernment - wise evaluation of what is true, what is appropriate and what is for the highest good, both for yourself and for the planet. In many ways discernment is similar to judgment. However, you will know when you are in judgment and when you have moved out of your heart when you are in a place of blame.

We know how challenging that this planet can be. We know how very real the illusions on this planet appear to be. We understand the incredible density of this dimension and the pressure you will face. But if you survive this mission - and it is a voluntary one - you will evolve at hyper speed.

We also should say that we know that some of you who go to this planet as starseeds, will never germinate - never awakened to the remembrance of who you really are. Some of you will awaken and begin to shine, only to be choked down by the opinions and prevailing thought forms around you. Others will awaken and remain awake and your light will become a source of inspiration and remembrance for many.

You will incarnate all over the planet; in every culture, every race, every country, and every religion. But you will be different. You will never quite fit in. As you awaken you will realize that your true family isn't those of your own race, culture, religion, county or even your biological family. It is your cosmic family - those who have come as you have come - on assignment to assist in ways large and small in the current transition.

As you pursue this mission there are only three things to remember: Who You Really Are, Why You Are Here and What This Is Really All About. You can do this by continually dwelling in the temple of Divine Presence, your heart, where this remembrance takes place and from which you are called to serve the world.

So, are your ready? Good!

Oh, and by the way, there are a couple of other minor things I should mention...

Because of the density, you can't operate in that dimension without a space suit. This is a biological suit that actually changes over time. There are many things we could tell you about this but our orientation time is short so I think you can just jump in and experience it. You should be forewarned, however. There will be a danger that if you forget who you really are, you may think you ARE your space suit instead of the fact that it is simply your vehicle in that dimension.

Once there, you will notice that there are an infinite variety of space suits and a great deal of attention given to these. However, in spite of the infinite variety, because this a planet of duality, they all fall into two basic categories called 'genders.' Again, we really don't have time to go into this now. But you will find your relationship with your own space suit to be most instructive and interesting.

The other little thing is this. In order to operate in that dimension, you will also receive a microchip called a 'personality.' This is like an identity imprint that, along with your space suit, will essentially make you different from everyone else. This will allow you to participate in the hologram there - something they call 'consensus reality.'

Once again, there will be a real danger that you will become so engrossed in the holographic personality dramas that you will forget who you really are and actually think that you ARE your personality. I know it sounds rather unbelievable right now, but once you get there...

Again, there is so much more we could tell you by way of orientation, but we think you can learn the rest experientially 'on site." The only thing that is important is to remember Who You Really Are, Why You Are Here and What This Is Really All About. If you can do that, everything else will work out fine. But take note: So few really DO remember this they stand out as 'different' and others called them 'Enlightened" or 'Awakened" and similar terms. Strange isn't it?

Well, Good Luck & Bon Voyage!!!

A Message From Big Mama (December 28th, 2004)
You know something? I'm kind of fed up with you guys. You take everything so personally. It doesn't occur to most of you that I am alive. Yes, I'm a living being just like you. I'm continually evolving, growing, changing, etc., and you are a part of my growth as you are a part of your own process. When I stretch, yawn, hiccup, sneeze or simply celebrate my Bat Mitzvah, you think it's some kind of collective punishment for your 'sins.'

We Need To Talk!

Your popular human religions have done you a deadly disservice by teaching you that I and all my other creatures are simply objects that were designed for your pleasure to use, abuse, exploit and destroy. Did it ever occur to you how arrogant that is?

We Need To Talk!

46

You worry about 'Earth Changes' -- no such thing except for the fact that I am continually changing. It's not an event. It's an ongoing process that you don't understand because of your fruit fly mentality.

Last week some guy found fossilized footprints of a dinosaur that roamed the suburbs of Washington, DC. 100 million years ago. That was long before you were even a suggestive sparkle in the Creators eyes.

Did you know that the total life span of a fruit fly is seven days? Seven days!

OK, so lets say this guy John-the-fruit-fly is born one Monday morning in late October. On Thursday, the first freeze of the season hits. John tragically freezes to death. Now one could take a fruit fly perspective and claim that this was some kind of punishment for Johns many fruit fly misdeeds or - taking a somewhat larger view of the matter - one could see that John had the unfortunate bad luck - or chose at some level - to be born four days before the first killing frost. John really doesn't understand time or cycles. His lifespan and genetic memory are too brief to grasp either one.

Do you have any idea how old I AM? Your life span isn't much more than that of a fruit fly. Your whole species is created, thrives and becomes extinct while I'm enjoying a cup of tea on a lovely cosmic afternoon. It's just that you don't have an 'eonic' sense of time so you tend to take things personally.

We Need To Talk!

One hundred years from now, you and everyone you know will be 'dead'.... and on to greater adventures. All the important people and events that you read about in the newspaper or see on TV... Gone, and for the most part, forgotten. I will still be here, yawning, hiccupping, sneezing and enjoying my afternoon tea long after your species ceases to even be a memory around this place. Put your petty daily dramas into **that** perspective.

Why does it always have To Be About You? Did it ever occur to you how much of your energy and money is focused on killing other species on this planet - and I'm not just talking about bug spray and chicken farms. You are spending over $175 million dollars a day to destroy Iraq while 14,000 children starve to death every day. That means that more children have starved to death so far since 12/26/04 - just from neglect - than all of those who died in the big wave. And then you applaud yourself for sending two days worth of war costs for relief. Now that is something you should take personally.

Yes, I'm pissed – Big Time! But God & I haven't conspired to punish you. You seem to do a fairly good job of that yourself. I'm just fed up with taking the blame - along with God - for just being who I am and doing what I have been doing for the last umpteen millions of years; long before you came on to the scene.

And though I may not sound very compassionate at the moment, I do feel the pain of every one of my creatures who suffer. Did you know that I sent a warning to let everyone know that I was about to sneeze? Did you see the news? The only ones who heard me were the wild animals in India and some 'primitive' tribal people on a remote island. They all went to higher ground just before the wave hit and none of them died. Why didn't the rest of you hear me???

So I let you know I'm about to sneeze, you don't hear me because you aren't listening, and it wreaks havoc. And then you have the audacity to blame God! Give me a break.

Maybe you should just start listening... Or even better, maybe you should ask yourself what you are doing that is so important that you aren't listening....

We Need To Talk!

Are You Suffering From PMT? *(November, 1997)*
The year was 995 ad. Western Europe; kingdoms and fiefdoms struggling to emerge from the dark ages. Anxiety was rampant. Only five years to the end of the millennium. The second coming of Christ and the end of the world was imminent. Wandering prophets were prolific, adding a touch of thrill to a very dull day-to-day existence.

Fast forward. The year is 1997. Three years away from the end of the second millennium. The prophets of doom still abound, having reincarnated as newspaper reporters, publishers and media moguls. Spiritual prophets are equally plentiful. But this is the age of equal access.

We are offered not only the Christian option of rapture, but the equally exciting technological option of being beamed up by an ET mother ship to escape the pending pole shifts, earth changes and world wars.

Since prophecy is "in," I'll add my own two cents. A long time ago I received a secret and special revelation that I have kept to myself until now. It may surprise and perhaps even disturb you. It's not the conventional wisdom in new age circles. But this isn't the first time I've flirted with heresy.

There won't be a pole shift in the year 1999 or 2,000. No major earth changes. No mother ship on the White House lawn. No rapture. No Armageddon. The year 2,001 will be business as usual. Surprised? Disappointed? Fearful of pending boredom? Sorry. That's the prophets' job, to call 'em like you see 'em.

What you may be experiencing - suffering from - is the recently identified PMT syndrome: Pre-Millennium Tension. It occurs at the end of each millennium in the western "Christian" world. People get a little tense, a little crazy; start saying and doing things that they often look back on and regret in the year 1,001 or 2,001. Common sense takes a nap.

Having said that and, hopefully stirred up some "stuff", let me say this. We are in the midst of profound and accelerated planetary transformation; socially, politically, technologically, spiritually and geologically. This change is accelerating. By all appearances we are moving rapidly toward the recognition of our galactic citizenship.

The keynote of galactic citizenship is r-e-s-p-o-n-s-a-b-i-l-i-t-y: personal and collective. With PMT there is a real temptation to blindly follow political, social or spiritual movements or leaders which claim to have all the answers and which offer salvation in one form or another - if only we play "follow the leader." From what I can see, this is about as old as old consciousness gets. It's also a dead end.

If Millennium Three is to truly be different than Millennium Two, we must move out of our personal and collective sense of victim-hood, discover how we participate, consciously or unconsciously, in the creation of our individual and collective reality, and assume full responsibility as co-creators of our world.

If a new era is to dawn, we must discover and learn to work with the Divine Presence, Wisdom and Power within ourselves, as ones created in the image of God, and to qualify all we do with Love, which is the Divine Will.

Political, social and religious movements can't and won't save us from ourselves. Too often they are as much a part of the problem as the solution. Playing "follow the leader" was a Piscean age game that won't create the world we want in the Age of Aquarius. This is a do-it-yourself age that is dawning. But the "yourself" is that divine aspect of self that is eternal, ever present, ever wise and ever creative. It is love expressed as joy - the kingdom within.

We are entering a new era - the era of possibility & responsibility. What it becomes is what we choose to become, consciously or unconsciously, individually and collectively. Becoming fully conscious and in resonance with the Divine Presence within is the only cure for fear and it's offspring, P.M.T.

PS: One hundred years from now, you and virtually everyone you know will be dead. Period. That may happen very quickly or it may be over a long period of time. So What? Also, perhaps a million or ten million years from now, the memory of this human species won't even exist on this planet. So What? The only important thing is the following questions:

The Morning Questions
* What makes me happy?
* What excites me today?
* What am I proud of in my life right now?
* What am I enjoying most in my life right now?
* What am I committed to now in my life?

The Evening Questions
* What have I given today?
* In what way have I contributed today?
* What did I learn today?
* How has today added to the quality of my life?
* Have I used today as an investment for my future?

Fundamental Questions
* What is my life really about?
* Why am I here?
* Am I really on the right track to fulfill my destiny?
* If I continue what am doing, in the next ten years what will become of me?

There is no yesterday, no tomorrow. Only Today!

Decisive Moments (February 18, 2008)
Each of us has those moments in our lives that are particularly decisive. We are standing at a crossroads. Before us are two pathways. Which path we choose will put into motion a set of events that will set the course of the rest of our lives.

Of course, at the time, we may not realize how decisive the moment really is. But then again, is not every moment and every decision such to some degree?

Looking back over my own life I can see the many decisive moments I had and the decisions that I made and – with hindsight – the consequences of those decisions; how they have affected my own life over the course of the years and how they have affected the lives of others, of family, friends and even strangers.

We are all children. Our species is still in kindergarten. We cannot see the effects of our decisions even two days in advance, much less two years, twenty years, seven generations or a dozen lifetimes.

If I had known at the time how my decisions would set the course of my life; how what I said and did would affect the course of other peoples lives; especially those closest to me, there are many things I would have done or decided differently. This is the dubious benefit of age and experience. The wrinkles are exquisite portraits of past experience.

But this isn't a litany of regret. The past does not exist except as a thought in those six inches between our ears. The past is beneficial only to the extent that the wisdom of experience informs the present & tempers the future.

That experience can become our Guide or our Warden. Too often we allow our past to become our prison. We can never escape the trauma of our past experience. This is stuff of which phobias are made. A traumatic experience creates a template of fear, anger or prejudice that we automatically and unconsciously overlay on every future experience. And in the process, we gradually become prisoners of the past. We no longer have the freedom to encounter life experiences with joyful, childlike freshness. Every experience carries the weight of a thousand past experiences with the same person, or someone that that person or experience reminds us of. We have become prisoners of the past. We bend low and age rapidly under the weight of our own baggage.

The wrinkles tell the story. It's not just about our diet or too much sun or sagging muscles. It's more about our sagging Spirit. They can be held a bay for a time. They can be removed for a season and a price. But they will return. Our wrinkles are the calligraphy of our experience. But the story they tell is personal. Is it the story of imprisonment or the story of wisdom?

It is the story we are writing each day of our life, including this very moment. But is it the endless-loop thinking of a prisoner whose mental world is a tiny cell of experience defined by the past, a sense victim-hood and reactive thinking, or is it the story of wisdom, informed by the past but defined by the freedom of the moment and proactive thinking?

My personal world started imploding in 1979. I lost my job; my relationship was on the rocks. My family was coming apart at the seams. I was sinking in a morass of self-pity. My own pain blinded me, not only to the pain of those around me – especially my wife & children – but also to the fact that I was **not** a victim and that this nightmare was something originating from within – not from without. I became a prisoner of my own pain and as the pain grew my world became smaller and smaller and smaller until it finally brought me to my knees.

And that of course is where I had to arrive – to rock bottom – before I was able to begin the journey Home. It was only when I totally collapsed in surrender on the stone floor of my dungeon that I discovered the key to the lock that let me escape. It was only when I collapsed in exhaustion from the terrifying pursuit of the nightmares monster, that the monster bent down and gently handed me the key that allowed me to awaken from the dream. And the irony is, the key was there all along; on the floor of my dungeon and in the hand of the monster. But I could not see it, blinded as I was by my pain, my fear, and my anger. It was only when I quit struggling and collapsed in total exhausted surrender that I found it.

And the key was this: just a simple realization. However much all of my problems seem to be the result of situations, circumstances or people 'out there' – this was a lie. The source was within myself. If I wanted to change my world I would have to change myself.

This realization was at once exciting and frightening. It was exciting in the fact that changing myself was one of those very few areas of life that I felt I had at least a little control over.

I had noticed that I could barely manage the outer situations and circumstances in my life, much less change them – and even that took enormous energy. And forget about people. I had learned long before that I wasn't going to change any of them!

So it was exciting to know that the only person that I really needed to change was ME and when I changed, like magic, my circumstances, situations and even the people in my life seemed to change.

Wow! This is pretty cool! It was a lot more fun and lighter than struggling to control, manipulate and change other people, circumstances and situations in my life, that's for sure.

But I found there was also a down side. I had to make some sacrifices. For one, I had to totally give up my self-pity. I had not realized how much self-pity had become my treasured companion and how much I loved theatrics. Oh how I loved to play the noble martyr, the victim. How much I enjoyed telling folks how I had been wronged by others, especially at my job. And yes they all agreed with me – they were my friends, right? We had this unspoken agreement that they would listen to my tales of woe and support me if I would listen to their tales of woe and support them – as long as we both never ever told each other what we were really thinking. After all, what are 'friends' for?

Anyway, as I was saying, there was a down side. I had to give up my self-pity and I had to give up my righteous indignation of being 'wronged' by others or the experiences or circumstances of life. In short, I had to sacrifice the luxury of blame. This was hard. Judgment & blame was in my DNA. If something bad happens, it has to be someone's fault. There has to be someone to blame – even if it's myself!

The key of assuming full personal responsibility for one's life isn't about transferring the judgment and blame of others to judging and blaming ourselves. It is about analyzing and understanding how our experience, beliefs, attitudes, decisions and actions have conspired to create the situations and circumstances in our life and how we can consciously change those, within ourselves, and create different outcomes; ones that are more in harmony of what we want in life.

As long as we are focused on trying to change others or constantly reacting to their behavior, we are not free. We are still prisoners.

As long as what another person says or does causes us to react; when they can 'push our buttons' or 'pull our strings' then we are merely puppets and they are the puppet master.

This is the situation of 99.99999% of the people of the world 99.99999% of the time. So we have plenty of company.

But does it bring us the happiness we seek or are we simply unconscious? We can choose to be the cause; as a creator who is in control of our own life or we can be the effect and subject to all of the swirling situations, circumstances and people around us. To see which we are, we only have to look at our decisions. Are they reactive or proactive?

In fact it was the biggest lie my Ego had concocted to keep me imprisoned. When I woke up to this realization it was like I had been asleep for eons – dreaming this nightmare from which I could not escape. Slowly I began to realize the extent that this Lie had totally dominated my life – how much I had really believed the nightmare was real life.

So if my challenges in life are not the result of situations, circumstances or people 'out there' then what are they?

I am of the school of thought - or perhaps I should say the deep seated knowing – that our only purpose here on Earth is first and foremost 'soul growth' or the expansion of consciousness that comes with the deepening awareness of our interconnectedness to All That Is. Our primary venue for such growth is learning to live by design and not by default. Stepping into our power of becoming conscious creators. This is the sum total of what it means to be created in the image of God – the Ultimate Creator.

To this end we have given ourselves a good dose of complete but temporary amnesia. We have created this elaborate theater we call the third dimension, put on these costumes we call our bodies and stepped into these characters we call our ego and personality. It is upon this stage that we have chosen to play out the dramas and learn the lessons implicit in the plots we have chosen. And it all proceeds in dead seriousness and with total amnesia.

To use another metaphor, we are like the dogs at the racetrack. After the count down they are released to run lap after lap around totally consumed with chasing a metal rabbit! Poor creatures! They think they are there to catch the rabbit. To this end they devote their obsessive attention and expend their total energy. How different are we in our day-to-day lives than the greyhound dogs?

We continue around the track, lap after lap, chasing our metal rabbits of financial security, relationships, love, healing our childhood, seeking the acceptance of others and a thousand other illusions we believe are the source of happiness.

Whether we are caught up in a nightmare, playing out the dramas of daily life or running the racetrack chasing our metal rabbits, the Ancients tell us that there is a way out. We can wake up from the nightmare. We can step off stage and see the drama for what it really is. We can stop dead in our obsessive thoughts and realize that all of the metal rabbits we are chasing are just that – metal rabbits. In that moment, whenever and however it happens, everything changes! Our world becomes new. Possibilities that always existed but were never available, suddenly appear. The magical world of synchronicity is ours.

But here is the catch. Most of us never stop long enough to see through our self-created dramas or to press pause on our obsessive endless-loop thinking, to find our way out. The adrenalin high of the drama is just too rich, the metal rabbits too alluring, the endless loop thinking groves too deep. We keep on doing what we have always done and we keep on getting what we have always gotten and we keep on wondering 'why this is happening to me again and again."

It is not until the excruciating pain has brought us to our knees and total collapse that we begin to consider that perhaps there is another way; another path that will bring us lasting happiness and true fulfillment and not simply the bright flash and energy surges of the ego highs we have experienced in the past. No, it doesn't have to be this way, but this is the way it seems to be. With some pause and reflective thinking, this alternative is always available to us but it seems to take the motivation of unbearable pain to push us over the edge. And even then 99% of the people seem to be able to hang on to the edge with a thousand ways to numb the pain. They are the walking dead....

The second road is much narrower and not so easy. It is the high road and carries the higher frequency of Spirit. If I choose this road then I will see the my adversary like a parent who sees a child throwing a tantrum - a child who is in deep pain, feeling rejected, bewildered, scared and hurt. I would also see through all of the ego drama into the heart and essence of a beautiful soul who has not discovered it's own beauty.

If I took the high road I would assume personal responsibility for having co-created the existing situation - not blaming the other person or myself - but realizing that we both created the situation by the choices we made.

If I took the high road I would not allow the other person's choices to pull me down to the low road, because I would be the master of my own journey. I would act rather than react. I would have responsibility for nothing but managing my own frequency and my own journey. I would have no need to win but only to find win/win solutions to common challenges. The signposts on this road are compassion, kindness, generosity, cooperation, respect, trust, honesty & love. And these are also its destination. The few times I have stepped out of my ego pain and taken this road, it has led to Bliss.

If I don't consciously choose my destination, then my first knee-jerk reaction is to take the first road, the road of ego. This is the broad and easy road and it's the only road that most people know.

If I choose to take this road then I would be very offended at what the other person did and said. My first response would be to retaliate with hurt for hurt. I would see myself as a victim and the other person being totally at fault. I would have a need to be right and the other person to be wrong. I would talk to all my friends and try to get them to be on my side just to prove to myself that I am right and the other person is wrong. I would need to win and have the other person lose. I would need to feel superior and the other person inferior. I would need to dictate what the other person should do or be according to my own ideas. I would get a certain satisfaction in revenge -- wanting the other person to feel the hurt that I feel. The signposts on this road are anger, hatred, mistrust, dishonesty, disrespect & fear. It is a low road because it carries a very low frequency. It is the road of war, constant battle and never ending conflict. I have taken this road before, and even when I have "won" a battle, it didn't bring me peace, joy or true satisfaction.
It left me empty because ultimately it was a dead end. The irony is that I never chose this road consciously because I never really consciously chose the destination I wanted to reach.

Each road leads to a different destination. It's not really a matter of good and bad or right and wrong. It's not even about the other person. It's a matter of being very clear about my desired destination in life and choosing the road that will take me there. The basic question is "Where do I want to end up?" Once I have decided that, I can choose the road that will take me there.

The Musings Of A Minor Prophet (April 6, 2001)
The "Land Of Jerusalem" stands at a crossroads. This Is A Historic Moment. Have you wondered why the Israelis are doing what they are doing to the Palestinians? Is it because they are naturally an aggressive, greedy, or hate filled people? Or is it because they are living in a deep state of the inner terror of annihilation as a people and as a nation after finally fulfilling the 2,000-year-old dream of returning home?

Have you ever wondered why the Palestinians are doing what they are doing to the Israelis? Is it because Palestinians are just an evil people and terrorists by nature? Or is it because they are reacting to what they see as foreign troops occupying their land, demolishing their homes, killing their children, and denying basic human rights?

Young Israeli soldiers don't shoot Palestinian children for the fun of it. It is born of deep-seated fear. Each time they do, something inside of them dies as well. They will never be the same.

Young Palestinians bombers don't blow themselves up because they enjoy suicide. It is a desperate act by desperate young men who have given up hope in life itself and of bringing about change any other way. And then there is the revenge factor.

Until each side ceases to see itself as the "innocent & virtuous victim" and the other side as the "evil demon incarnate"...

Until both sides begin to see the humanness of each other; the deep suffering of the other; the legitimate longings and the justified grievances...

Until this happens, the violence will continue and will escalate.

Both sides have experienced more than enough atrocities.... And perpetuated them. How much more pain and suffering must both sides endure before everyone wakes up and realizes that the current course of action is not working to produce what each side wants?

How many more children must both sides sacrifice to the false gods of fear and hatred; how many arms, legs and eyes lost, before people are willing to change; before the majority of people on both sides wake up and say enough!!!

Both sides claim that the violence is only in reaction to the other side. But all of the outward violence is the product of the inner violence of attitude on both sides. Until this changes, the children will continue to die.... On both sides....

Israelis and Palestinians, as historic brothers and the children of Abraham, have the opportunity to offer the whole world a model of cooperation, justice, peace and prosperity. The Palestinians can have Justice and the Israelis can have Security. Both can have Peace & Prosperity. But neither will have what they want until they are willing to grant these to the other.

Jerusalem can fulfill its destiny as an international model of peace and brotherhood, governed by its own citizens, or it can once again become a city of desolation and despair. This is its fate if everyone doesn't wake up - and very soon.

The frequencies of anger, hatred, revenge and fear are being anchored in the land itself. When these stresses become too intense, the Earth will release them. She will tremble and land will roll like the waves of the sea. She will not distinguish between Palestinian and Israeli; between Christian, Jew or Muslim. All will pay the price and in the silent aftermath, they will call it "The Judgment Of God."

This is not the fate of Jerusalem, and it need not be a step toward the fulfillment of its Divine Destiny as an international model of peace and brotherhood. If everyone wakes up now from this nightmare to remember who they really are, why they are here and this beautiful vision of The New Jerusalem, then everything can change in the twinkling of an eye.

Awaken The People Now! Let the Guardians of Light transmute the anger, fear and hatred, and release the tension from the Earth.

May the "Land Of Jerusalem" be preserved. May all of her people know justice, security, peace & prosperity. May we surmount our pain, our suffering, our history and our fears. May we create a glorious future and show the whole world what is possible when brothers live together in Peace. May a river of light again flow forth from Zion and bless the whole world. This is the destiny of Jerusalem. May it be fulfilled Now!

My Journey
(The following was written in 2003 at the request of my friend, Maggie Erotokritou, for her book Spiritual Awakenings: Glimpses into the Higher Realms published in 2005).

One of my earliest memories, around five years of age, comes to me strongly as I begin this writing about my spiritual journey. I remember being in my bedroom. I am holding one of my favorite teddy bears, dipping my hand in a bowl of water and baptizing him. At the time it seemed quite normal. As I look back upon it now -- being only five years old -- it was a more than strange.

Another vivid memory stands out. I was perhaps ten at the time. Our small family home had a full basement. In one corner there was a small, separate room, perhaps 8 x 10 feet that we called the coal room. Its original purpose was for storing coal for the furnace. But since we heated with gas, it ended up being a storage place for garden vegetables that mom canned and various other odds and ends.

One day I had the inspiration to create a place for personal devotion. With permission from my parents I cleaned out the coal room thoroughly and then set up a three tier alter at one end completed with an elaborate covering, candles, incense, etc. Many years later, in thumbing through a National Geographic magazine, I saw a photo of something quite similar, taken in one of the Buddhist monasteries in Tibet.

We were not a particularly religious family. The church in a small town in the South was simply a part of community life. You attended because it was the socially expected thing to do. You did it because your parents did it and their parents before them. Religion or spiritual matters were never discussed in the home. It was as if my personal zeal to devotion was something that I was born with.

And thus begins the story of my spiritual journey.

Unlike many individuals, past and present, I have never had an earth shattering spiritual experience. I've never had a near death experience, been blinded by the Light, been brought to my knees sobbing from profound suffering or the mystical experience of the oneness of the Universe. These are only things I read about.

No, apparently I have chosen a different path, a decision, which seems to mark my life. If there was a beginning point to my journey, it is lost in the mists of times and lives long past. I came into this current incarnation with 'things spiritual' as my dominant concern.

Water forms itself to the nature of the container. Spirit is much the same. The container I chose to begin the journey of this incarnation was a working class family of four in a small town in Kentucky. It was a secure beginning. I was often reminded that I was a 'planned child' and was very much wanted. My sister was eight years older and my parents very much wanted their second child to be a boy. Our home was small, but it was a quiet and orderly family. There was zero drama in the early years. It was not until I became a teenager, during the Vietnam war and the Civil Rights movement, that the drama with my father began. But that is another story.

Church, school and home. These were the three pillars of existence while growing up. Slowly, the Church became the dominant influence in my life. State Street Methodist church was one of the largest churches in town. It stood in stately stone, a block from the central plaza, it's arched gothic stained glass windows a timeless reminder of realms beyond our daily mundane pursuits.

We attended church and Sunday school almost every Sunday and, as I became older and could make choices, I often attended midweek as well. I plunged totally into the Church experience as an outlet -- or doorway -- for my deep spiritual promptings. I read the bible and took it all quite seriously.

This continued, quite unabated, through my teen years. By age 18 I had organized a group of adults from all of the Methodist churches in town to initiate a weekly visitation program to each of the nursing homes, bringing a bit of light and joy to the abandoned elders.

From there I began spending Sunday afternoon "across the tracks" gathering small groups of children in the yards of friendly neighbors, sharing Bible stories with them. Over the course of three years, this led to the organization of a new Methodist congregation in the neighborhood and eventually a new church building.

This was the kind of outlet for spiritual expression that was available for the circumstances I had chosen to enter. My own particular focus was service, not dogma or doctrine. I had very little interest in theology, dogma or beliefs. I always felt that action was more important than words.

As I now look back on those years I realize that the work I took on was simply the only outlet available, given my circumstances. But it was foretaste of things to come.

Needless to say, I was different. Though never openly discussed, I supposed that others views of me were quite varied; from that of my peers who may have found my zeal weird and perhaps threatening, to the dear old ladies of the Church who found it very noble and endearing. There was always an unspoken assumption that I would become a clergyman.

But they didn't know my secret.

Along with my baptizing teddy bears, one of my earliest memories -- again at around five -- was my sexual attraction/fascination with other boys. Psychologists and enlighten counselors will tell you, of course, that this is not uncommon. But, in 1950, no one was there to tell me this. My attraction to guys became my 'big secret.' It also became perhaps the most defining element of my life -- including my spiritual journey.

As I look back now, I often wonder if my zeal-in-service was some kind of unconscious attempt at atonement-through-good-works for this horrid sexual attraction toward guys. No, I would never become a minister. I was not good enough. Like St. Paul, I had a 'thorn in the flesh' -- some indescribable fault that could not be discussed but must be endured in suffering silence.

So with this, the split began. There was my mental life -- my sexual fantasies and, by my mid teens, actual experiences with peers - and there was my life that most people saw; a zealous young man endeavoring to imitate St. Francis. And between the two, there was a full-blown war underway. It was as if my own soul had become a battleground.

Too many questions, not enough answers. This wasn't a 'choice' any more than breathing or hunger. It was the way I was created. This much I knew. But I also knew (though I never remember it spoken of in the pulpit or elsewhere at that time) that it was 'wrong' according to our religious teachings.

In my ongoing battle I searched the bible and found enough scripture to back up my resistance to these 'unnatural urges' -- enough scripture to crucify myself on a cross of profound guilt. The silent suffering fit perfectly into my piscine need to suffer. If I was created this way and it was wrong, did God make a mistake? Does God create junk? Or was everyone else wrong? Too many questions, not enough answers...

And while I crucified myself silently with self-judgment, I projected it onto the others in our church. Hypocrisy wasn't too difficult to find in the southern church during the civil rights movement and the Vietnam War. Slowly I began to see the church in a different light, not as the vehicle of God's grace, but as a powerful guardian of social tradition that used the bible to back up it's very selective beliefs and used Jesus as a kind of spiritual mascot.

One particular incident stands out. Our church janitor, who was Black, had worked for the church 30 years or more. Since he worked on weekends at the church, he didn't have a real church home. So when he died, his family requested to have his funeral at the church that he loved and cared for, for so many years. Apparently the request had to be taken before the board of directors for approval and an intense discussion ensued; some fearing that if it was held there then it might alienate some of the wealthier members and the new air conditioner wouldn't get paid for. And although they did the right thing and it was approved, the very fact that it had to be discussed was a decisive turning point for me. I woke up and began seeing the church for what it really was and not the idealized vision I had of it.

My understandings are gentler now, but the intensity of the times and my personal inner war over my sexuality assisted me in my eventual graduation from the Church. I speak of having 'graduated' from the church. It wasn't simply a rejection but more that my questions outgrew the answers that were offered. Too many things simply didn't make any sense. But this didn't happen suddenly.

Other memories are quite distinct. I remember how strange I thought it was to see people pledge allegiance to a flag with 'liberty and justice for all', while being deeply offended by seeing separate drinking fountains and separate bathrooms for white and black people; how strange it was that my peers would shoot birds with their BB guns 'just for fun.' In fact, so many things I saw and heard seemed to be so strange and disturbing that I gradually developed a sense of not being from this place; not belonging here.

My view was global, my passion was service, and my circumstances were small town Methodist church. So each of these converged into a natural progression that led me to a decision to become a missionary.

I completed my first two years of college in my hometown and continued on to Nashville, Tenn. in 1967 to complete my last two years at a church college, in preparation for serving overseas. It was at this point that I came into contact with the Religious Society Of Friends - the Quakers.

My religious interests had me reading and exploring the world of ideas long before I left home. Very early on I found a natural affinity with Buddhism; one, which I came to realize later, was rooted in many past lives. In Nashville, I discovered the Quakers, already knowing their beliefs and much of their history.

The late 60's was an intense time. In the Quakers I found people who were unequivocally opposed to war, and in particular the Vietnam War. I personally met deeply spiritual and committed individuals who refused to pay a portion of their income tax which was being used for war. I met middle class, middle aged white southerners who were actively involved in the civil rights movement. I met a group of people who came together weekly to spend an hour in silence to "wait on the Light" of Divine inspiration from within rather than sermons based on the multitude of interpretations of scripture, external dogma and personal prejudices. In short, I had found a home.

In 1968 I was married. Julia was a Cuban refugee and a fellow student. She was also raised Methodist, which gave us some cultural similarity that we might not have otherwise had. By this time I was 23, I had left home, and had realized that there was a much larger world 'out there' geographically, culturally and with the world of ideas and beliefs. I also started to gradually come to terms with myself.

Given the way I was raised, in circumstances where nothing of substance was ever discussed, and considering my own inner struggles -- honesty became paramount in my life, at least with those closest to me. So before the marriage plans were laid, I told Julia that I had slept with guys, but never with another woman. Her feeling was that this was not uncommon for boys and once we were married, it would take care of itself. I wanted desperately to believe that.

The early 70's marked the arrival of kids, four in all. It also marked a gradual refocusing of energy more toward family and career and away from spiritual pursuits.

With three in diapers and bottles and a wife in graduate school, there was precious little time for contemplating the nature of the Universe. High ideals of 'saving the world' had to be replaced with feeding and clothing my own kids. That continued on through the 70's

Then, in 1979 I lost my job as the executive director of an urban neighborhood development program. It was a pivotal event. I had reached a turning point. The job, and particularly the politics involved, had become intolerable, but I didn't have the courage to walk out -- not with a family that depended on me financially and not enough confidence that I would find another job. So I decided to remain unconscious and simply orchestrate getting fired at other levels. This allowed me to feel and play the victim, which I did, complete with righteous indignation. Now I can laugh at it and see how it was so perfect. At the time it didn't feel so perfect.

As I said, I had reached a turning point. If I had continued and been willing to 'play the game' as expected, I would have ended up behind a corporate desk at central headquarters in another city. Instead, I chose not to play the game and ended up on my butt, thinking "What next?"

The 'what next' was a bold move. I returned to the area of my true interest; human consciousness. Within three months I opened up the Human Potential Institute, a very nice sounding name for a clinical hypnosis practice. This was Nashville, Tennessee, 1980. Not exactly a hotbed of progressive thinking. How that all came about is a story in and of itself, but not directly pertinent to my spiritual journey.

What is pertinent to my journey is what evolved from opening the Institute. Just the word 'hypnosis' has a way of attracting 'not quite normal' people, or at least those who were willing to look for life's answers outside of the box. So in addition to people, who wanted to lose weight, stop smoking or deal with other challenging habits, there were others who wanted to explore their childhood through regression or other interests even farther afield.

The Institute became a magnet for those with alternative interests, and once again, I began to see a much larger world than I had known - the inner world of human consciousness and potential beyond religious dogma and beliefs or even the enlightened perceptions of the Quakers.

It was at this time that I discovered reincarnation, and quite by accident. I supposed I had read about it since, by age 35 I had read a great deal about many philosophies. But I didn't have any conviction about it one way or the other. That was before a series of experiences in which several of my clients, who definitely didn't believe in reincarnation, had profound, vivid and descriptive past life recall under hypnosis. Over time, with more reading and hypnotic research, an understanding of the continuity of life from incarnation to incarnation became one of the cornerstones of my knowing.

It was about the same time, 1980, that I discovered what was to be the next path on my spiritual journey. My vision for the Human Potential Institute had always been larger than simply a clinical hypnosis practice. I wanted also to offer leading edge workshops and seminars. So when the opportunity to host a Native American 'medicine man' came up, I jumped at it. Steven Old Coyote was of the Cree tribe, raised among the Lakota of South Dakota and living on the Olympic Peninsula of Washington State. He was a representative of the XAT Medicine Society, a pan-tribal organization dedicated to bringing back many of the traditional teachings, which were appropriate for our times.

Meeting and listening to Old Coyote was like finding a missing link to a spiritual connection that I had felt since early childhood, but had no context for understanding. It was the spiritual connection to nature. Christianity was a human religion and largely 'Western' – culturally speaking.

The Quakers, however exceptional, were a part of that tradition. At the time, they all spoke to the human condition only. The Earth, as everyone knew, was an inanimate object, given for man's domination and consumption. At the very best, we were to be good 'stewards,' but the relationship was one of ownership and dominance. Something deep inside of me knew that there was something wrong with this picture. But, as with so many of my innate knowings since childhood, this was weird and I didn't know anyone else who shared this understanding. So I had long kept silent, even as I had begun to spend more and more time alone in nature and less and less time in Church or religious gatherings, Quaker or otherwise. The trees, clouds, streams, birds, wind -- even the nature spirits which I could feel, though not see -- became my companions and teachers.

And then I met Old Coyote and it all came together. As I began to study the Native American spiritual path I began to realize that this is what I had always known. It was like rediscovering what you had lost. And I plunged into it deeply. We formed a local medicine society, came together monthly to drum, sing, pray and do ceremony and to explore together. As I came to meet other teachers who visited our group and others associated with XAT, I came to realize that in many ways, it wasn't a great deal different than the church.

Human ego is human ego, regardless of the belief system it embraces. There was just as much ego, just as much need to control, just as much personal inconsistency, just as much bickering and dogma and drama among 'medicine teachers' as there was with garden variety Baptist. However, following this path for several years did reconnect me to the Earth at a spiritual level and provided a foundation for the next step.

My inner Guidance was becoming stronger and clearer. By 1989 I had started receiving strong inner promptings related to angels, a subject which had never particularly interested me before. Growing up as a Protestant, angels didn't play a significant role in religious teaching, except as a relic of the past. But I kept receiving this inner urge to find and learn the names of the seven archangels and to invoke their assistance.

All of this was quite strange to me but I had learned long ago to follow Guidance, at least after enough resistance to determine that it really was Guidance and not some passing fancy.

It was about this time, in 1990, that I began to notice an inner shift from my focus on Nature based spirituality to 'celestial concerns.' It was if I had been gently guided into some kind of spiritual weaving of heaven and earth with the meeting point being the human heart.

Many things were happening concurrently during the late 80's and 90's. In 1986, at the urging of a friend, I organized a small psychic fair, mostly as a fun event and because I was known as an exceptionally good organizer and trusted by the many psychic friends I had made through the Human Potential Institute. It went much better than anticipated and everyone wanted to know when the next one would be.

I had no intention of becoming a promoter of psychic fairs. While I maintained an ongoing interest in the anomalies and unanswered questions of human consciousness, I had no personal experience with psychic phenomena and must confess that I held to some of the common prejudices of such stuff being more appropriate to carnivals.

But being one who has always fought prejudice, it became apparent that organizing such events was my next piece of curriculum. These 'Festival's Of Light' as they became known, continued for 12 years and brought me into contact with many interesting people and ideas. I also learned the difference between psychic and spiritual.

August 1987 saw the advent of the event known as the Harmonic Convergence, an event that -- according to some -- was connected to prophecies from the Mayan calendar. It marked the end of one age, a 26,000 year cosmic cycle, and the beginning of a new era. History will determine the truth or fantasy of such a claim. However, for me personally and for many others I knew, it was a turning point. Something had come to an end and something was beginning.

It was as this time that I started receiving the first glimmers as to who I was, why I had chosen to be on the Earth at this time, and what I was here to do. I refer to it now as the time that I consciously received (or remembered) my assignment.

The main thing I remember was having a vision of a series of world maps. The first map was totally black. The second map had a few small points of light here and there. The next map had more points of light and they were larger.

The following map had more, larger points and a few were connected by lines of light. This process continued until the last map was completely white. I was inwardly told that this represented the 25 year transition time from 1987 until the year 2012, and that my job during this time was to 'connect the dots.'

I was 'told' that the time was soon coming when people would have questions that the traditional custodians of the answers (religious, political, educational, medical, scientific) would not have answers for. I came to understand that there were people all over the world, from every continent, every country, every religion and race who had come to the Earth at this time to play a midwifery role during this transition. These were the points of light. These were the ones I was to identify and connect. That was it. No details, no 'how to' instructions, no budget, nothing.

This was crazy, I had a family to support and I didn't have the kind of resources or contacts that allowed me to carry out such an assignment. My first reaction was to try to find someone else to do it. Having failed at that, I simply put it out of my mind and resisted the whole notion for a little over a year.

Finally, in the autumn of 1988, under intense and consistent inner pressure, I gave in. By this time I had started to identify some of the emerging grass root leaders of the so called 'new age movement.' They were the growing number of publishers of such magazines and newspapers. I sent a hundred letters of invitation to those whom I had identified throughout the USA. Twenty responded affirmatively and a month later we convened a network gathering at a small camp near Nashville, Tenn. For three days we sat together in a circle and shared. There were no speakers, no workshops, and no lectures. We came together as peers simply to get to know each other, to share our story, our perspective and to explore ways of working together.

I had no agenda personally other than fulfilling an assignment. At the conclusion of that gathering I felt that this had been done. Little did I know. The group wanted to meet again... in three months!

Thus began what, for a year, became quarterly network gatherings. I stepped back from leadership and in fact didn't attend the third one in the summer of '89 because I was leading a tour group to Peru at the time.

By the autumn of that year the gatherings began to falter. I had reached another turning point. Decision time. I had set my sights in more practical directions, geared to earning a living, a pursuit that had become an increasing challenge. An October gathering had been scheduled but the person who was to lead it was trying to cancel the gathering. I was contacted by some of the participants and urged to reassume leadership.

Three weeks earlier I had broken my leg in a very freakish but providential way. With my leg in a cast, I had every right to say no. I was on the phone to a friend who was to become my primary spiritual advisor/advocate. She was basically haranguing me about how important it was to attend and reassume leadership. In the midst of her long monolog, I simply and quietly said, "OK, I will go."

Every aspect of my being knew that this was a decisive moment, not unlike the day I was fired from my last 'real job." It set the course for the next phase of my life and work. One that would have been very different than if I had said no. So two days after I had the cast on my right leg reduced from my hip to just below my knee, I got in the car, cast and all, and drove five hours over mountainous roads to the retreat center where the gathering was held.

This meeting laid the foundation for what was to become the "Light Links" and "Light Summits" which began in 1990 in Sedona, Arizona and continued at a regional, national and international level through the final one in Jerusalem in 2001.

The network gatherings were just one attempt to fulfill this assignment of connecting the dots. In 1992 I put together the first 'International Directory of Light Leaders' followed soon after by an 'International Directory of New Age Newspapers and Magazines' and then an international newspaper called "Planetary Connections.'

I was as a man possessed; single minded in my commitment to 'planetary transformation.' But somewhere along the way, my connection with my family slipped away. Like far too many men, especially "Type A's," I was married to my work. I loved my family but my devotion was to my work. When Julia completed her Ph.D. and took a university teaching position 500 miles away, it was agreed that I would remain in Nashville until our son completed high school and she was securely settled with our youngest daughter in her new position. That took two years.

In the autumn of 1991 we sold our house in Nashville so that she could buy one in her new home in Pennsylvania. I still had things to wrap up in Nashville so I got an apartment and remained until August 1992.

These were intense years; 1986-1992. It seemed that change was relentless. I felt possessed by the "hound of heaven." Perhaps it was so. Perhaps it was only a way of not dealing with deeper personal issues. But whatever it was, it was intense. It was at this time that I experienced two deep infatuations (both with women), let my hair grow long (which I had missed doing in the 60's) and legally changed my name.

It all culminated in August 1992 when I left Nashville, after 25 years, and moved -- not to Pennsylvania - but to the mountains of western North Carolina. Julia and I never really 'broke up.' We didn't divorce. Something simply dissolved, more or less gradually. Her move in 1988 was simply the culmination of a process that had begun many years earlier, a process that I assume most of the responsibility for.

One of my most cherished dreams, from the time of my late teens, was to live in a small secluded cabin next to a mountain stream. In my mind it was one room with a loft. At one end there was a large stone fireplace with bookcases on either side. A big front porch and plenty of rocking chairs -- a retreat in nature, where I feel most at home. Moving to the mountains was returning to my first love; nature, serenity and freedom.

But the opportunity to fulfill one's dreams, especially by changing geographic location, can be one of life's greatest lessons. We generally find "there" what we experienced "here" because the reality 'out there' is simply a reflection of the reality we carry within.

My move to the mountains didn't fit my childhood picture. The reality was an older rented house, shared with a good friend, in a working class neighborhood at the edge of town. Moreover, my Type A behavior only intensified. I became a virtual prisoner of the various projects I had started. The newspaper alone quickly became the proverbial "tail that wagged the dog." Periodically our bathtub would be occupied for a week at a time with 10,000 newly printed newspapers waiting to be shipped all over the world. Things started imploding by the end of 1994. More shifts were happening.

I turned the paper over to others who had a passion for it, and as I did, I received a very clear message from within. It said, "From this point forward, for the rest of your life, whatever you accomplish in the world will not be the result of anything you do.... But who you are."

How simple and yet how profound. It went on to explain that there would continue to be plenty of doing, and this was OK, but the real effect I would have in the world would be the result of who I am, not what I did. For an obsessive workaholic this was about as profound as profound gets. It also marked what was to be the beginning of a three year period of inner retreat that was to last until early 1998.

In October of 1995 circumstances conspired to offer me the opportunity to actually buy a secluded and dilapidated cottage in the mountains. With little skill and less money, but a lot of energy, I accepted the challenge and moved, spending the next several years living by myself and remodeling the cottage.

Others found my living alone in the mountains a bit strange but I felt that I had found heaven. With the exception of a few months here and there since leaving home, it was my first time of really being alone. I loved it. More importantly it offered me endless hours in nature, away from the frenetic energy of the city. It offered me the opportunity for listening more to the voice within than the outward chattering of consensus reality. I came to understand Thoreau.

It also laid the foundation for my next step. In the spring of 1996, after spending regular times each day in quiet meditation, I received the prompting to write down what seemed to be a conversation I was having with myself or an aspect of myself.

Though I was never comfortable with the term channeling, it probably best describes the experience. About six months into it I was asked (inwardly) to put certain parts of it together into a book. Again, resistance. These channeling's were given to me and for me. It was very personal. It wasn't given for public consumption, or so I thought. So being clever, I offered a bargain; "You come up with the money and I will put it into a book.' Ha, I thought, that should take care of it. One of the things I had noticed since losing my last job was that money didn't exactly grow on trees.

And then I was approached by a friend who had been impressed with the channeled information I had shared with her and offered me the money to publish a book. The angelic ones had the last laugh. Thus was born "A Day Of Grace," a book of daily reflections taken from the channeled information I had received in 1996

It still continues to be my personal guide. The bottom line of the whole thing is Love; it's about opening one's heart. This I have come to see is the goal, at least for me and for the next few lifetimes. There is no doubt that I have accomplished a great deal in the world of "doing." Many successful projects, many lives touched and changed, much to my credit in the world of doing. But what about the world of being? I have always contended that if you want to really know a person, ask those closest to them. In my case, my children, my wife, my parents (now deceased) and my housemates.

The period of personal retreat came to a close by the end of 1997. Most people never knew it was happening because the outward projects continued. Another shift was in the making. As I reassumed a lot of responsibilities and took on additional ones, I made the decision to move my communications and networking totally to the Internet.

70

In the mid 80's I was told by Guidance that the time would come that I would be living in a cabin in the mountains and running an international communications hub for 'lightworkers.' I was also 'instructed' to create an international 'planetary emergency alert system' in which hundreds of thousands of light workers could be mobilized in a matter of hours to bring their interdimensional skills to bear on critical world situations.

At the time, that was not conceivable since the only means of communication was the telephone and fax. And then came the Internet. For an international networker like my self, it was a godsend. No longer would I have to wait months for the exchange of letters with co-workers in Africa. It was only a matter of hours or days.

In February of 1998 I received an email appealing for people to meditate for peace regarding the Middle East situation and the USA's pending invasion of Iraq. And then I received another one from someone else, and then another and another. I received 30 in all of the same email, which was being forwarded back and forth among those who had an interest in such things.

This triggered the idea that we would all benefit from a system where one person could send something to everyone at the same time and we could eliminate the duplication. I wrote those on my email list and posed the idea of setting up an association of networks for this purpose. The response was positive and immediate. Within two weeks we had over 150 networks registered. This later became known as the Planetary Awakening Network. By the end of 2003 there were more than 1,000 networks from 60 countries that had registered to participate. It was only after a few weeks had passed that I suddenly realized that I had fulfilled the instructions I had received over ten years earlier about creating an 'international planetary alert system' and my office and laptop in my mountain cottage had indeed become an international communication hub.

Those who are closest to me, know how profoundly human I am. And, like each of us, there are things I would do very differently given the chance, especially with my family. I would be less the possessed doer of projects and more the appreciator and cherisher of what and who I had in my life. It is a matter of living with an open heart. Saving the world is easy. Talking spirituality is even easier. Opening your heart totally and being vulnerable and fully intimate with those closest to you; being honest with yourself and others; retaining the innocence of childhood without being naive and having the wisdom of many years without becoming jaded, this is true spirituality.

I am reminded of a dream I had in 1984. I had spent much of that year intensely studying dreams. Toward the end of that period I had an unusual 'dream.' It wasn't the normal dream that involved images or some kind of drama. It was a voice, a very clear voice that spoke to me just before I woke up. It said, "In the end, you will be judged, not by the gods in whom you believe, but by the quality of your love." It was clear that it was not how much we love but how well. Also, the statement carried a double meaning. We would not be judged by God nor by our beliefs, but by the quality of our love.

As with a few other experiences in life, this was a major turning point. It was the dissolving of the final chain that bound me to old dogmas and beliefs. I came to understand that our beliefs were of the mind. They only existed in the six inches or so between our ears and they would dissolve with our brain tissue in the grave. Only the quality of our love would survive and that would determine nature of our journey between lives and the beginning point of our next incarnation. This understanding became, and continues to be my personal guide and goal: to open my heart.

If I were still a conventional Christian I would be very frightened, not because of hell or other such fantasies, but for fear of not getting it all done in just one life time. Coming to understand the ongoing nature of life as a cyclical event of incarnations has liberated me from knowing I have to get it all done now. I know that all I have to do today is to remain awake and remember who I am, why I am here and what this is all about. Some days I succeed and some days I don't.

In the spiritual world, contrary to what the major religions teach, one size doesn't fit all any more than one department or course of study is appropriate for all students in the University.

Some people have found it beneficial to have a spiritual teacher or guru. Others find benefit in following a particular religion or spiritual path rigorously. I am reminded of what one of my Native American elders said, "The only valid question is 'does it grow corn.' In other words does it work? Being something of a rascal, he went on to say "if standing on your head Thursday night and eating crackers does it for you, do it!"

I am reminded that this accepting perspective probably accounts for the fact that, while they may have fought over hunting territory or ponies, Native Americans never fought over religion. Each person was responsible only to the Creator for his spiritual welfare, not to the dictates of another human or the dogma and laws of a book.

I have walked upon many spiritual paths beginning with an artful blend of Protestant Christianity and small town southern culture that was the backbone of the Methodist church. This provided both the foundation and a somewhat conservative reference point for further development.

The Quakers were a major influence that spoke directly to my heart and essential knowings. The Native American path reconnected me to the spiritual essence of nature, even though I soon found that the exacting rituals and 'stones & bones' part of it were little different from dogmatic churchism. Buddhist and Taoist teachings have always touched my soul as well, though I have never been involved in formal study or practicing groups. The delving into the vast realm of human potential certainly merged into and raised many profound spiritual questions. The call of the angelic realms, channeling and such have played their part as well.

But I have found that, for me at least, the real gurus of life have been life itself. It seems that my ego, my relationships, my sexuality, my relationship with money, and my body -- all of them have provided me with more than enough curriculum for personal and spiritual growth. I have no need to travel to India to find an enlightened teacher. I am surrounded by teachers who are present to shine their light onto and into my life, if my eyes are open to see it. I call it 'God in drag; the One appearing as the many.' I have also been blessed with honest friends and family members who gently and sometimes not so gently help me see my blind spots.

I even came to see the grace of my flexible sexual orientation. I eventually realized that all organized religion was based upon at least as much cultural tradition as it was upon the teachings of its founder. I realized that God doesn't make mistakes or create junk. I realized that I chose my curriculum before I came into this life and my sexuality was a part of that. What I did with it was my choice as well.

I am not seeking 'enlightenment' nor 'salvation.' I am not waiting for the second coming of Christ nor to be rescued by a mother ship. I am only seeking to remain awake and to remember; to remember who I am, why I am here and what this is all about. If I can do that, moment-to-moment, it is enough. I seek only to keep an open heart, one moment at a time. If I can do that, it is enough.

I seek also to remain alert to the whisperings of my heart. I have come to learn that it is there that the voice of God speaks to me most clearly. Beyond this, I have few convictions.

There are three ways of looking at everything; 'I agree', 'I disagree' and 'that's interesting.' The older I get the less I embrace or reject and the more I simply accept things as interesting or worthy of consideration.

My journey hasn't been particularly easy, but I am grateful for the entire curriculum I have chosen. I am grateful for the many lives that have touched my own and the lives I have been able to touch. I am grateful for the lessons learned and the bits of wisdom that experience has granted me.

Above all, I am grateful for the peace I have attained with Divine Presence. There is a gentle intimacy that stands outside of religion, ceremony, the need to appease, placate or manipulate. I do not claim that my way is THE way. It is simply my way. But above all, for me at least, it grows corn.

And, like all of us, I am still a work in progress. As of this writing I am in the process of releasing many of my long-term projects to others as I watch my life moving into new endeavors. Recently a friend asked me about my beliefs on a certain subject. After giving a very definitive answer, I laughed and went on to say "but don't hold me to any of this next Tuesday. I may learn or experience something that will cause me to understand things differently tomorrow, next week or next year." Life is fluid. Flowing gracefully with these changes is a part of the Grace we receive in life.

Reflections on the Middle East (March, 2001)

A few weeks ago I shared with my cyber network something I had received regarding the internationalization of Jerusalem as a "holy city of peace." I was graced with dozens of responses, 95% of which were supportive of the idea. I was also accused of being a tool of Zionism, a tool of the PLO and a tool of the New World Order – all of which I took as a collective compliment to what I like to think is a degree of objectivity.

Among my many pursuits, I am a farmer. Farmers, by nature, are very practical people. As all farmers around the world know, whether the family eats or not depends on whether the crops grow. Good farmers understand the importance of working with the laws and forces of nature. The bottom line question is always "does it grow corn?"

My own corn crop wasn't so good this year and I already know why. But I didn't learn this bottom line principal from the other farmers in my valley. I learned it from my Native American elders many years ago. One wise teacher taught me this basic truth: "The only important question is, 'does it grow corn." Perhaps it is time that we had more practical farmers as leaders of nations.

As I look at the situation in the Mideast I see the dramatization of an "old world order" which is both bankrupt and dysfunctional. If I were to speak metaphysically and macrocosmically I would say that the people in this region have taken on the enormous and admirable burden of showing the rest of the world what doesn't work.

I have visited Israel/Palestine many times and have close friends in both communities. When the recent crisis began in October and quickly escalated into unspeakable horrors, it was like a knife in my heart. I could literally feel the pain, despair, outrage and fear of all of the participants. It would not be truthful to say that I have emotionally disengaged from this situation completely, but I have come to view it from other perspectives besides the immediate suffering which is so apparent.

Like most things in my life, however painful, I try to find the lesson or greater understanding. The ongoing Mideast drama forcefully reminded me how much each of us are prisoners of our beliefs and it is from those beliefs that we individually and collectively create our – sometimes very painful - experience.

The responses I received to the Jerusalem Declaration were a predictable reflection of the individual and collective truths or myths of each respondent.

As I look at similar situations in Northern Ireland, Kosovo, Rwanda, and a dozen other places around the world, I see how ethnic and religious violence is perpetuated by the beliefs/truths/myths we hold about our adversaries and ourselves.

The problem is, of course; too often these truths/beliefs/myths simply don't grow corn. They don't help us produce what we all say we want: love, peace, security, health, justice, prosperity, and a healthy planet. It would be difficult to find an Israeli or Palestinian who does not want exactly this for themselves and their families. The same is true for Protestants and Catholics in Northern Ireland, Serbs & Albanians in Kosovo or Hutus and Tutsis in Rwanda.

So what prevents us from having just that? Could it be that our passionate ethnic or religious beliefs are of greater value to us than human life or love or peace, security, health, justice, prosperity, and a healthy planet. As we look at the world, one is inclined to think so.

But these beliefs/truths/myths that we carry in the six inches between our ears have little to do with Ultimate Reality. Because Ultimately Reality grows corn.

This brings us to the biggest, deepest and most fundamental question which haunts both our personal and collective life as a species: "How much pain & suffering are we willing to experience - individually & collectively - before we are willing to change?"

How long will we live with the illusion of victimhood; that "they" are the source of our pain and suffering? How long must we suffer before we wake up to the reality that we are the authors of our own experience: if not deliberately, then by default, and that our beliefs are the blueprints from which we create.

It has been my observation that Divine Presence allows us all the experience necessary, including the pain, to bring us home to the ultimate and only reality - Love. When we arrive at and can remain in that place, it becomes a fountain that sustains all other aspects of our life.

Even as we do what we can from a human perspective to alleviate suffering in the Mideast and elsewhere, let us also honor the great sacrifice which both sides in this crisis are making to show the rest the world in a dramatic way – what doesn't work.

It seems that it is only when we have charged repeatedly head first into a brick wall, and repeatedly suffered the predictable consequences, that our minds are finally opened to more creative options to getting to the other side of that wall. How does the saying go: "If we keep on doing what we have always done, we will keep on getting what we have always got."

The Ultimate Guru

Seeking a wise teacher in the caves of the Himalayas or a wizened shaman in the Andes or Amazon is always an option. Certainly we have long held a strong attraction to "the exotic other" as a source of wisdom and enlightenment. However, in our ongoing quest for a deeper understanding of ourselves and our world, we have often failed to recognize the Ultimate Guru in our lives.

This "Master Of All Masters" wears no robes. There are no sonorous chants in ancient languages; No hidden teachings to tantalize the seeker; No rituals, ceremony or hierarchy of believers; No special relationship with ascended beings; No occult techniques, formulas, prayers or meditations. The truth is, this "Master Of All Masters" is the most unglamorous and mundane guru one could possibly imagine: So much so that she is always overlooked in our attraction to "the exotic other."

Who is this "Master Of All Masters" - This Ultimate Guru? Relationships. Yes, just that: Simply relationships.

Our magnificent world offers a wondrous array of "the exotic other" in terms of teachers. There are all kinds of gurus of various sorts and types. Each may have a teaching to offer at the various stages of our lives and journeys into consciousness. But when we have walked the many byways to enlightenment, ultimately the last path will bring us back to where we started. Relationships.

When we hear the word Relationships, our first thought is often "romantic." But this is but a tiny fraction of the whole; like only the big toe of the guru.

Consider all of the relationships in your life: Your relationship with your body; your relationship with money; your relationship with The Divine realm; your relationship with your own beliefs, your relationship with your own personal myth of who and what you are; your relationship with your home; your relationship with the Earth.

And then there are people: Your relationship with your spouse, your children, your parents, siblings, friends, enemies, coworkers, and strangers - and of course your romances. And there is that relationship with the intangible "Self" - the who and what you truly are at the deepest core of your being. Indeed, what is your life and who are you but your relationships in the very broad sense of the term?

And how is your relationship with each of these? Are you consciously working with them or only learning indirectly and by default? Are you journeying to exotic inner and outer destinations and ignoring the Ultimate Guru at your doorstep? Are you ready to embrace her in all of her homely mundane worldliness and make this a truly conscious adventure this time around?

It is said that we teach what we most need to learn and that to understand the issues in another's life, look at what they are teaching.

I don't pretend to be a teacher, for truly, I have no teachings. And as for beliefs, don't hold me to them next Tuesday. Something may occur this weekend that will give me a greater or deeper understanding of Life.

But a guide, yes. I have walked many of the paths I have alluded to. In the early 90's, with my own tour company, I was leading pilgrimages to the ancient sacred sites of Earth. Early in life I embarked on the marriage and family path. In 1995 I moved to a secluded mountain sanctuary to explore the path of a solitaire - to pause and look at my many relationships in life. I've learned a few things along the way and I have many yet to learn.

But this one thing I know. I have learned - and continue to learn and grow - more from the relationships in my life than from all of the books in my library, all of the scriptures I have read, all of the religions I have studied and all the guru lectures I have heard. While they have all been helpful, my greatest growth has come from that ultimate guru; from the experience of relationships; from the grinding together of ecstasy and agony and from the intensity of the grinding.

Where Is The Gift?

In 1979 I was fired from my position as the executive director of Neighborhood Housing Services in Nashville, Tennessee as a result of a policy dispute with the board of directors.

At the time I was immersed in the idea that I was a martyred victim of a vocal minority who had swayed the board to take this action. I was hurt, angry, indignant and fearful of the future, as well as stubborn and pigheaded. I had also been extremely unhappy with the job for over a year and didn't have the guts to quit.

This move catapulted me into a whole new arena. In the midst of my searching for some form of independent income, I came upon one of the myriad multi-level marketing programs that I embraced enthusiastically. Well, I didn't get rich - at least not materially - but I tapped into something that has brought me more wealth than I could have imagined in 1980.

Each week for months we would come together at the home of our sponsor for a pep talk. In retrospect I see that it was a training class in the law of attraction prior to these ideas becoming popular in the spiritual community and the media.

I learned that the Universe operates in accord with our individual & collective beliefs and attitudes. I came to realize that I had incredible creative powers to determine my future within the framework of the collective belief system and sometimes outside of it. I had heard some of these concepts before but I had never integrated them into my life.

The cornerstone of this system of reference was an understanding that "In every seeming adversity there is the seed of an equal or greater benefit." That's right. I don't care how bad it is, if you will look close enough you will find the seed of "an equal or greater benefit" in the situation. Because it is a seed, it may take time to manifest, but it is there. Simply put: "Every challenge carries a gift."

I am acutely aware of the suffering in the world and I don't write lightly about this. When we are among the trees it is hard to see the forest. However, it is only from a cosmic perspective, or often "down the road" a bit that we can bring things into perspective and see the real benefit of a situation or circumstance in our individual lives or in the life of the world.

It all begins with attitude. I once heard a 60-year-old motivational speaker open his talk by saying that nothing bad had happened to him since he was 40 years old! That certainly got my attention. He did admit that a number of unpleasant things had occurred and each time he said to himself "that's good, where's the gift?" And then he went about finding the good and the gift in it. He said he was invariably successful. Pollyannaish? Some would say so. To counter, he would say plain and simple that it works. This has been my experience as well. It works.

The Universe supports our every belief and attitude. If we want to feel we are victims, we have that freedom and people will constantly abuse us. We also have the freedom to reframe each of our experiences and see how they have helped us to stretch and grow in wisdom and maturity. It's our choice.

There is an advanced philosophy that states that circumstances are essentially neutral. It is our beliefs and attitude that give them meaning. And it is the meaning we give them which causes our emotional or physical reaction. A simple example is food. Certain insects and snails are considered a delicacy by some and would cause mouth watering. Others would retch at even the idea of eating these.

The Creator has given us a beautiful playground called Planet Earth. We have been given the ability to co-create with our lives and our world. Are your current beliefs and attitudes increasing your joy and happiness, your prosperity and love or are they causing you pain?

God In Drag (Channeled Guidance received in 1998)

Mikael, we are here once again, an emissary of the Divine Light. We are here in the full power and presence of the I Am that I am that you are. We come to you in joy, we come to you in light, we come to you delightfully. We come to you from beyond the farthest reaches of reality, from beyond the edge of infinity, beyond the edge of eternity. And yet we come to you from the very deepest regions of your own heart. Indeed we have never left you, for we are always a part of you. We are an emissary of the I Am that I Am that you are. We come to awaken in you that remembrance of who you are and why you are here and what this is really all about.

So, who are we? We are not, as we have said, an entity, we are not this ascended master; we are not that commander of a galactic fleet. No, we are the I Am that I Am that you are. We are of you. This is why we say to you that we cannot tell you anything that you do not already know. We can only remind you of who you are; perhaps nudging you out of that corner of consciousness that you dwell in day after day. We call you into the place of remembrance, into a remembrance of the Oneness and the Unity of the I Am that I am that you are.

How do you move out of this microcosmic corner of your consciousness, of this drama that you dwell in, day to day? How do you move from that into the expanded understanding of your true nature? It is through your heart. The vehicle that carries you is love, pure and simple. So we bring you here, not to teach you. No. We bring you here, not to give you new information, for indeed, what can we tell you that you cannot find in books? What can we tell you that you cannot find in your own dreams? What can we tell you that you cannot find as you move into a place of remembrance? No, we bring you here to soak in this hot tub of bliss. For even as you soak in a hot tub, your tired and tense muscles relax, so when you soak in the hot tub of bliss - into the presence and the remembrance of the I Am That I Am that you are - your heart opens. When your heart opens, the world is transformed. As we said before and we say again, it is not what you do that will bring about the transformation of your planet, it is who you are. It is who you are. It is the energy of your heart.

So we invite you into that heart space. We invite you into that place of remembrance of the I Am Presence that you are. Allow the brilliant light of the I Am that you are to ignite and illuminate your heart center. Allow that Light to grow and fill your entire being, radiating out from you and over lapping with those around you until, indeed, you create a cosmic heart. Within this cosmic heart all of the little dramas of your life can be consumed. This Cosmic Heart will shine with such radiance, such brilliance, such joy and such love, that all of the little dream dramas that you so easily become trapped in, within the template of duality, all of them simply dissolve in the brilliant light of this cosmic heart energy.

So perhaps we titillated you a bit when referring to this evening's conversation as "God in Drag". It brings a smile to your face. We would give you a different way of looking at your world; a different way of viewing your daily drama.

There are those in your life that you have had issues with: business partners, old loves, parents, children, employees, employers and friends who have betrayed you. Who are they? Who are they? They are God in Drag.

We come to you in a myriad of ways to bring you to an understanding of your true nature and the true nature of reality. Some of you learn quickly and some of you learn very, very slowly. And when you are a very slow learner, what happens? You have to continually repeat the lesson until you master the subject. The same drama, different actors. But who are those actors in your drama? The good guys, the bad guys and the irrelevant? Guess who?

You would not believe the wardrobe that we have of wigs and dresses. We can come to you in ways that you cannot imagine. We can make you laugh, we can make you cry, and we can bring up every emotion that you know and some that you haven't met yet. All for the purpose of helping you to remember who you are, who you really are. We have a thousand ways of dressing up and coming to you to awaken from the dream drama and into Reality; into the template of oneness.

You can abandon your friends and family and go to foreign lands in your search of God. You can go to India or Tibet. You can go to the ancient sacred sites of Mexico, Egypt, Peru or England. You can go to the great gurus, the great teachers, there is nothing wrong with this. But it is that business partner that cheats you, it is that lover that does not live up to your expectations, it is that overbearing parent, that thankless child, it is in all of these that we come to you day by day to awaken you to who you really are.

For indeed, we are in drag and every moment you are given the choice for your heart to expand and incorporate each experience, expand and incorporate each person in your life from the macrocosmic prospective, or to contract and reject. It is the energy of love or it is the energy of fear. This is not the first time you have heard that it is always a choice between love and fear. No. It sounds so easy, and yet we say that, as we observe the workings of your life, it is only when you move from the tiny corner of your consciousness that is locked in to the template of duality that is so deeply involved in the drama; it is only when you move out of that into an understanding of your higher self, into the I Am that I Am, that you are - it is only then that you can truly open your heart to love.

Now you are often instructed concerning fear, that fear is something bad, if it were something bad it would not have been created as a part of your life package. Fear is good. It is good that you are fearful of burning your hand if you stick it into a fire. It is good that you know that there are certain things that are unwise to do because you will no longer exist in the third dimension if you do them.

It is good that you are fearful to run a red light in rush hour traffic. Fear can be, and is, a good thing to preserve you physically. It does have its purposes. But when you let it run rampant and dominate your entire existence, the results are what you see in the present, what you see dominating your world today. Fear was meant to be an instrument for preserving the physical vehicle, not a tool of the ego.

Now let us share a secret with you. You have been told that there was a time in the dark past of your creation that you were cast out of the Garden of Eden for having disobeyed God. You were told that this god was like an angry father who punished his children harshly when they disobeyed. You were taught that sometimes he even hated, was furiously angry and even required blood sacrifices. In fact, he had every human emotion.

We say to you this: This god that you learned of was a human creation. This is the god of your nightmare, this is the god of your own construct; constructed in your nightmare. This is not the Creator of the Universe. The Creator of the Universe, the Source of All That Is, is so far beyond your limited imagination and conception that in the shadow of such a Presence you are utterly speechless. Divine Presence is NOT the collection of human emotions and attributes and to claim such is nothing short of idolatry.

You were never cast out of the Garden of Eden. You only fell asleep and have been having this terrible nightmare of this tyrannical god. We tell you, for we are of the I Am that I Am that you are, the All That Is, is simply Love. As you awaken, truly awaken from this nightmare you will find that you are still living in the Garden of Eden. When you awaken from your nightmare, your life becomes so beautiful, so filled with joy, so blessed that it is beyond words.

As you entered this dimension, you went straight into amnesia as to who you really are and why you are here. Soon after you were born, you fell asleep, as it were, and began to dream this collective & fear filled nightmare. And for many of you it brought such deep sadness, such deep pain.

But that time is over, we have brought you to this place of awakening. You have come to this place of healing and - slowly for some and rapidly for others, little by little - you are waking up and rubbing your eyes and remembering, "Yes, this is the garden." You are beginning to remember who you are, remembering why you are here and remembering what this is all about.

Visualize now a column of light before you. We are inviting you to offer into this column of light those parts of yourself that you wish to release, perhaps those alienated parts of yourself that have not been brought into the light. Release into this column those parts of yourself that you would like for your Higher Self not to look at.

To the extent that you are ready and to the extent that you are able, release these into the light and allow the transmutation & transformation to take place in this moment. For the energy of this light is the energy of all the masters, of all the guides and all the angels and archangels, it is the I Am energy, the energy of love.

There is no condemnation, there is no judgment, there is only a deeper awareness, a deeper understanding, and a deeper awakening. As you touch into this, allow your heart to open more and more to those parts of yourself that need embracing, those wounded parts of yourself, those alienated parts of yourself.

Allow the I Am to love, to enfold, to heal, to nurture and bring you to the point of ascension. We are working with you now energetically, in moments of silence. We are working with you at the frequency level to create an opening; a greater capacity for Love. Yes.

You have found yourself at times being like a ping pong ball with your consciousness bouncing from the microcosm to the macrocosm, from the dream drama to the full understanding of who you are and seeing the world from the I Am Presence that you are. So we are saying that you are going to begin to spend more and more time in the macrocosm.

You are going to spend more and more time seeing things from the big picture; from the larger understanding. And yes, you will still catch yourself from time to time in the drama, talking about others, caught up in the negativity and the fear. But this time you will be aware of it, whereas in the past you would have been unconscious of it. So you are on a journey from the microcosmic perspective to the macrocosmic perspective. You are on the journey from being a victim of your circumstances to being the conscious creator of all that is within your life. There is so much beauty, there is so much grace, there is so much abundance that awaits you. It is as if you will fly on a magic carpet to worlds that you never dreamed of.

Now perhaps there is a question? Perhaps there is an answer that needs a question? Good, we enjoy games; we like to play the question/answer game. But we know, and we think you know and understand, that we are that of you which already knows; that already has the answers, even as you have the questions. We are that part of you that understands that there is a level of consciousness that transcends questions and answers. Nevertheless, we can playfully entertain your so-called questions.

Last week we spoke to those gathered saying that, Mikael has holes in his socks. Each of us, - and we say "us" as we are expressed through each individual, for "you", "us", "we" is all one. Each expression of consciousness as it manifests in the third dimension, ego personality, each has holes in its socks. Those imperfections that are hidden to others and sometimes even to ourselves. So we would ask you to look within yourself and see who is riding the magic carpet, for indeed the ego cannot hang on tight enough.

Let us give you an illustration. Imagine a triangle inverted with a point down and about 10% of that triangle sticking below the surface of the ocean, the other 90% sticking above the ocean. That 10% that sticks below the surface of this body of water, is your personality, ego self; that part that you are locked into most of the time, the dream drama part. That is the part that struggles with relationships, that is the part struggles with finances, that is the part that struggles with all of the drama. That part cannot ride the magic carpet.

We invite you to move into that 90% of who you really are; that which is connected to everyone and everything; that which is the I Am Presence. That part is all-powerful. Consciously allow the power and authority of that 90% of who you are to dominate your life and you will soar on the magic carpet of Love. When you surrender to the 90% of who you are and allow that part to dominate and run your very existence then all limitations and all obstacles will be removed. Can your ego surrender control? Can it allow you to step out of your petty dramas? To do so is the very key to your liberation and bliss.

You have heard it said, "I am the way, the truth and the light, no man comes to the father, but by me." There was a great misunderstanding here because this was attributed to the personality of Jesus; Rabbi Yeshua Ben Joseph. It is the I Am presence that you are, that spoke these words through him.

The I Am that I Am that you are is the way, the truth and the light. No one comes to the Source except through the I Am that you are - that within yourself; it is not found in another person – and we cannot stress this enough - it is not found in another person, it is not found in another religion.

Whatever the religion, however beautiful the person, how ever great the teachings, however dynamic the spiritual movement, It is not found in these. No, it is found within yourself. So you can say, even as Yeshua Ben Joseph said, I am the way, the truth, and the light, no man comes to the father, no person comes to the source but though me. And what is that which speaks? It is I Am that I Am that you are. It is not the personality or ego. Do you understand the shifting into that part of complete power within you that creates and dis-creates?

We would invite you now to the experience of Love. Can you remember a time when you held a child in your arms, or perhaps a puppy or kitten? Holding that fragile innocent life in your arms and allowing your heart to open completely as your love flowed to that small one? So now, experience that again. Not only the love flowing from your heart but allow the Love from Source to pour into the top of your head and flow through your heart.

Direct that love, like a beam of light from your heat center to those people and situations in your life that need love. And remember, as we have said before, it will not be the words, the teachings, the books you read or all the good deeds that are done in the world that will bring about a transformation and awakening, but it will be who you are. It will be your love. It will be your love.

As your love embraces your own fears it will transform the monsters that have haunted your life into the cherubs that fly about you in joy. As you allow that love to enfold and transform these shadows so you will become a purer, finer instrument of Divine Presence.

The Keys To Eden (Channeled Guidance received in 1998)
What I say to you is of no consequence whatsoever. What you experience of me, within your self, is the only thing that matters. So I call you out of that place of your mind. I call you out of that place of your ego. I call you out of that place of your personality. I call you out of that one percent of yourself and I call you into your heart.

I call you into the experiential part of yourself that I Am in order to experience that part of me that is manifested in and through most of who and what you are. And as you step sideways, just ever so slightly, into that ninety nine percent of who you are, you will find you have no challenges. You will find you have no problems, you will find the love that you have been seeking outside of yourself; you will find it in me. And where am I but within you, as you? For I Am the love that you are.

How many times will you need to trip and fall face first into the mud before you will cease journeying to the four corners of the world looking for that which is within you; the I AM that you are? And I am love. If you could see with the clear vision and complete perception, at all levels and in all dimensions, you would see how even now, you are so totally enfolded in wings of love, in wings of grace, in wings of beauty and in wings of joy. And as I speak to you of this, it is not to deny the fact that the one percent of who you are is experiencing anger or some other ego-based emotion.

Let me give you a picture. Imagine you are the parent - a parent with a two year old. You may remember that this is a particularly obstinate age of "I will do it my own self." OK, you have the picture. As a parent you would enfold the little one and protect the little one from the little hurts. But the little one has to do it "his own self" and so, being the grand and benevolent parent that you are, you allow him the experience, knowing where it will lead.

And when she runs up against the pain and turns around to run into your arms, your arms are open and the band aids are ready and you are ready to kiss the "ow, ow".

I Am that I Am that part of you that is of the all that is. And when you are ready to surrender the insistence upon doing it your own self, whether it is your financial life, your relationships, your health or any other aspect of your life; when you are ready to totally and completely surrender, my arms are open. And I will enfold you in a love that is beyond your wildest imagination.

I am that ninety nine percent of your reality. You will never, ever, be able to experience a love or a joy greater than that which I Am. You will not find it in a religion, you will not find it in a spiritual path, and you will not find it in a guru or a teacher. You will not find it in a lover.

Each of them, as they touch different parts of your life and your need for love; each of them are but a very dim reflection of My Love. They are no more than a small birthday candle compared to the blazing sun of my Love and my Presence. How much pain and frustration do you choose to experience before you surrender totally to my love? My arms are wide open. In me there is no condemnation, there is no judgment, there is only love without conditions, for that is who and what I Am.

The irony of it all is that when you come to this place of utter, total, and complete surrender to my Love, your experience will not be limited to some kind of celestial, spiritual or etheric love. My love is manifested through every aspect in your life; through every person, every situation, circumstance and experience. When you surrender to my Love, then my Love begins to radiate from you and like a magnet draws love in all forms to you. As you become the Presence of Love in the world, others will be competing to be with you. There will be many warm arms and warm hearts wanting to hold you.

Do you understand what I Am saying to you? You have said, "I want this person, I want that person, I want this job, this circumstance in my life". And there is nothing wrong with that. You can spend your life perusing that. It is good to have intention for you are here to learn to be a master of the material world. And part of your mastership is the experimentation of what works and what doesn't work.

Let me give you another picture, you are the three year old. And you are standing on the bank of a swiftly flowing creek. Now maybe the water only comes up to your ankles, but you can't quite see the bottom. And there are big rocks and there are small rocks and it is a bit treacherous. Now you can be the "I will do it my own self" and start across the creek and there will be times when you will slip and fall, perhaps, and bruise yourself. And each time you do, each time you experience this pain, of course, you will learn something from it.

We are not saying to stay safely in the arms of your parent. We are saying to cross the creek but don't be obstinate. Take the hand of your parent. Allow your loving mother to hold your hand and guide you across the creek. You were not meant to do it alone, except as you choose to do it alone.

Do you understand the pain that I feel as you feel pain? Because of the way you have been taught you see Divine Presence as something as far above and remote from you, perhaps not even concerned - but if concerned, still out of reach.

I Am saying to you that the pain you feel, I feel because we are one. The difference is, you are attached to the pain and I Am not attached to the pain. With you the pain lingers, with your one percent expression, through the ego and the personality, the pain is stuck. But in that part of you that I am, that ninety nine percent of who you are, the pain moves through and registers and we are connected. And my love reaches out and enfolds that other aspect of myself that you are, even more.

When you reach the point in any aspect of your life; financial, romantic, health, whatever, and say, " I am at my wits end, I don't know where to go." When you become as a little child and truly let go and surrender to that part of yourself that I Am; at that moment you open the door for me to step through and into your life, expressing myself as that ninety nine percent of who you really are. In that moment magic happens and miracles occur. At that moment, all things converge for the highest good, both for yourself and all others.

How often, when you have desired something so much, whether it be another person, a material thing, a special kind of connection with someone; how often have you truly, at the very core of your being wanted what was best for that person? You see, this is the test of whether you are operating from the one percent or the ninety nine percent reality of I Am that you are.

That one percent of you wants to fulfill its ego desires and attachments whereas the ninety nine percent of who you really are understands the Oneness of All and seeks only the highest good. And there again is the irony. The ego fights and struggles to have its way and in the process, experiences a great deal of pain. And all the while, if you had simply shifted into the Higher Self of your true nature, you would begin to see magic and miracles unfold.

This is the key to Eden. For what is Eden in your mind, except paradise? And what is paradise in your mind, except the state of being in love, totally cared for, totally enfolded, totally provided for. And the doorway is simply surrendering the egos will to the highest good.

And again I say to you that the creation, the specification and the definition of your intentions and desires are good. But when this is done, bless them and turn them over to your Higher Self for the manifestation. Release your attachment to the outcome.

And remember this, there is nothing wrong with the one percent of who you are. This is a part of your reality. This is also Divine Presence interpenetrating into the third dimension as an individual energy in a state of amnesia, and it is good. This one percent allows you to touch, feel and fully experience this 3D hologram. This one percent that comprises the ego and personality is like the colored glasses you wear at a 3D movie. It allows you to fully experience the illusion. So there is nothing wrong with this unless you forgot that it is just a movie.

So create your intent, create your desire and then give them to me on a golden platter. For I Am the one that will bring them forth in your life. Do you understand that the created part is that part of you that separates, defines, articulates and creates intent? This is a part of myself functioning in the creation process. That one percent, once it is done, has completed its job. It is not the job of that one percent to manifest that which has been divinely intended. Do you understand? It is then brought back, surrendered, turned over, presented, if you will, on a golden platter. And I then will bring forth the highest good. So this is your key, this is your key to Eden.

Call to mind a moment of time in your life when you felt most loved. It might have been by a parent. It might have been enfolded in the arms of a lover. In that moment call to mind the ecstasy, the total sense of warmth, security and protection that this experience brought to you. It might have been in the warm, strong arms of your grandmother or grandfather.

Whatever it was, bring that into your mind and into your heart now. And know that the love and security that you felt at that time is but a dim reflection of the reality of the love that I Am in your life. For in my eyes you are innocent and my love is without condition.

Now I would invite you to shift your reference point from that of looking outside of yourself for answers and guidance, to looking inside. Listen to the whisperings of your own heart – the still small voice within. Here I Am. Here I reside. This has always and will ever be my one true dwelling place. I Am that I Am.

Kissing Frogs
It's true, you know. We are reptilian. At the center of our three-part brain lies that original brain core scientists call reptilian. It is that instinctual part which worries mostly about food, shelter, sex and security - that looks out for number one.

Great wisdom is coded in our ancient fairy tales. One such story that appears in many forms in various cultures, is the frog-turned-prince-with-a kiss. The familiar scene opens with the handsome prince living under a cruel spell that has turned him into a frog. The spell can only be broken by the kiss of a princess; a princess who can see beyond the outer form to what lies within.

Our lives are full of frogs. At home, at work, in our social lives there are those we find loathsome. Perhaps we even find a frog staring back at us when we look in the mirror. Personally, socially, culturally we live under the wicked spell of profound pain born of fear.

Strip away the fear, strip away the layers of pain with a kiss and we will find a prince or princess. Criticize, judge, condemn and we add layer upon layer of pain and fear and push the hidden prince deeper and deeper into his frog costume.

Each of us posses the magic wand of personal and planetary transformation. It isn't more workshops, seminars, classes or gurus; it isn't the perfect religion or political system; it isn't great esoteric wisdom or magical skills. It is simply love. It is the ability to see into and through the frog-like fear and pain of another person, group of people, or even our self; into the essence of their princely nature and to touch that nature with the magic of love; to see as God sees.

Political tyranny, terrorism, war, crime and the great cruelties of our age are born of the same energy we experience in personal relationships gone sour; fear and pain. We live in a holographic universe. When we judge and condemn, born of our own fear and pain, we add to the sum total in the universe at all levels. When we choose to love; to see and seek to elicit the princely nature in another and act accordingly, we wield a powerful tool for transformation.

Several years ago I was in Jerusalem three days after the mosque massacre at Hebron. At one point in occupied East Jerusalem we came to an intersection with three trucks of Israeli soldiers; young conscripts with machine guns drawn. Scattered clusters of young Palestinians stood at a distance. Gunfire echoed down the street. The fear and pain that emanated from these young men - on both sides - was profound. My heart went out to the young Palestinians in their fear and pain of humiliation of living under foreign occupation. My heart went out to the young Jewish soldiers who are forced into the army and given a machine gun at age 18. It would be easy to blame their leaders and the politicians. But my heart went out to them as well.

I saw the fear and pain of Palestinian leaders who have felt that they had to turn to terrorism and killing innocent people out of the frustration and pain of 45 years of being refugees and being ignored by the international community; the pain and humiliation of being forced out of their homes at gunpoint and seeing their children shot down in the streets by foreign troops.

I saw the fear and pain of the Israeli leaders, born out of the holocaust, whose deepest fear is that of annihilation and whose deepest desire is for security to live in peace and prosperity; to return to their ancient homeland, rebuild their nation and to be strong as a people once again.

I saw the blindness on both sides in the belief that the only way one could win is for the other to lose; that guns could bring peace; that God favored one people above another; that true peace could be obtained by anything less than love.

In relationships, whether personal, social, international, or inter-dimensional, there are no "good guys and bad guys." That is an illusion of the ego. There are only good guys; some of whom have discovered their princely nature and some of whom are locked deep in the dungeon of their own fear and pain, believing themselves to be frogs and convincing others of the same.

We carry the key in our hearts to open the dungeon door; to transform the energy on the planet with thoughts and actions of love. One thought or act of love today toward one of the frogs in our lives will bring us closer to individual and collective ascension than all the rites, rituals or esoteric practices of all the world's religions and cults.

... Love...
Seeing the good in everyone
And helping them to see it in themselves.

The Bible Says That?

This is not written to be a criticism of the bible, the church or Christianity. Each of them have played a valuable role in my life, and I know that the bible, as well as the holy books of other religions is a source of guidance and comfort for many.

No, this is written both as a declaration of faith and challenge to those who call themselves "Christian" and would use very selective verses from the bible to terrorize people with fear, shame, guilt and judgment. It is a word of caution for those who take parts of the bible literally to back up their preconceived notions while ignoring or 'explaining' other parts which are inconvenient or inconsistent with their beliefs.

I was raised in a small town in Kentucky, USA. The church was a major institution in the community and in our family life. Biblical teachings and stories were a part of the culture. I was also very religious and swallowed it all "hook, line and sinker." I even went to a church college in preparation to becoming a missionary to work in the slums of South America.

But I eventually graduated from college, and from the church. I still honor what I learned from both, but I also see the limitations of academic knowledge and organized religion.

For me, the church was a kind of "spiritual kindergarten.' It was great place to start, but one that had a glass ceiling in terms of spiritual growth.

It all began in 1961, when I was 16 years old. We were an all white church, of course. Our Janitor (who was black) had faithfully served the church for almost 40 years. He really loved our Church and when he passed away, the family asked if they could have the funeral there. A Black man's funeral at OUR church?

There was a big debate on the board of directors. Apparently they were concerned that if they did, it might alienate some of the wealthy members and the new central air conditioning system might not get paid for. That was the starting point. I knew in my heart that something was wrong with this picture.

This followed soon after by watching the Church's response, or lack of response to our nation going half way around the world to bomb innocent civilians in their villages in the Vietnam war. It was then that I started realizing that organized religion - regardless of the brand - was primarily a cultural institution that reflected the common cultural beliefs of it's locale rather than the teachings of it's founder. As I have traveled, I have found this true around the world; whether it is Christianity (whatever brand), Islam, Buddhism, Hinduism, Judaism, Taoism or whatever. Most find it much easier to worship the founder or a book than to follow their simple teachings.

One of the things I have noticed in Christianity, with which I am most familiar, is that many people who say they believe that the bible is the infallible word of God and every word and commandment is true and unchanging, don't really believe that when you get into the details.

I have found that what they really believe are only those passages that are convenient or back up their preconceived notions. Those passages that are inconvenient are generally ignored or explained away. Here are some interesting ones one's that I have yet to see embraced by even the most literal interpreter of the bible.

Handicapped Clergy
Should Christians object to having a minister or pastor who wears glasses, is blind, or has some other kind of physical disability? Leviticus 21:18 - 23 clearly prohibits anyone who has a handicap from fulfilling all the functions of a priest - he cannot be blind, deaf, or have a physical impairment of any kind. He cannot even have an injured hand or an injured foot.

Food
Should Christians eat pork, rabbit, oysters, scallops, clams & shrimp? Leviticus 11:3-8 & Leviticus 11:9-12 clearly condemn this.

92

Farming & tailoring
Should Christians allow the breeding of different kinds of cattle, sowing different crops in the same field or making clothes with two different kinds of material such as cotton and polyester?

Leviticus 19:19 states clearly: "You shall not let your cattle breed with a different kind; you shall not sow your field with two kinds of seed; nor shall there come upon you a garment of cloth made of two kinds of stuff."

(A Word About Leviticus: It is interesting that this is the same book that contains the passages that are most often quoted by those opposed to same sex love. Wonder if they also believe the rest of the laws of Leviticus?)

Women
Should Christian men forbid women to open their mouths in Church?

1 Corinthians 14:34 states *"Let your women keep silence in the churches: for it is not permitted unto them to speak; but they are commanded to be under obedience, as also saith the law."*

Are women allowed to pray without covering their heads?

1 Corinthians 11:5 sates "*But every woman that prayeth or prophesieth with her head uncovered dishonoureth her head: for that is even all one as if she were shaven."*

Praying
Are Christian pastors and evangelist wrong when they pray in public - especially long prayers that are more like sermons?

Matthew 6:7-7 clearly commands *"But when ye pray, use not vain repetitions, as the heathen do: for they think that they shall be heard for their much speaking. But thou, when thou prayest, enter into thy closet, and when thou hast shut thy door, pray to thy Father which is in secret; and thy Father which seeth in secret shall reward thee openly."*

Should we really only pray in our closets? What if a person doesn't have a closet?

Marriage
It is acceptable for marriage to consist of a union between one man and more than one woman? (II Samuel 3:2-5)

Marriage does not impede a man's right to take concubines, in addition to his wife or wives. (II Samuel 5:13; I Kings 11:3; II Chronicles 11:21)

A marriage is considered valid only if the wife is a virgin. If the wife is discovered not to be a virgin, the marriage is considered dissolved and the woman is to be executed! (Deuteronomy 22: 13-21)

The marriage of a believer and nonbeliever is forbidden (Genesis 24:3, Numbers 25:1, Ezra 8:12; Nehemiah 10:30)

If a married man dies without children, his brother is to marry the widow. If he refuses to marry his brothers' widow or deliberately does not give her children, he is to pay a fine of one shoe, and be otherwise punished in a manner to be determined by law (Genesis 38:6-10; Deuteronomy 25:5-10

Is the only valid reason to get married is because you can't control your sexual urge? That's what Paul says in 1st Corinthians 8-9:

"I say therefore to the unmarried and widows, it is good for them if they abide even as I (single). But if they cannot contain their passion, let them marry: for it is better to marry than to burn."

Lending Money For Interest
Definition: Usury, from the Medieval Latin usuria, "interest' or "excessive interest', from Latin usura 'interest' was defined originally as charging a fee for the use of money. This usually meant interest on loans, although charging a fee for changing money (as at bureau de change) is included in the original meaning. After moderate-interest loans were made more easily available usury became an accepted part of the business world in the early modern age.

Exd 22:25 *"If thou lend money to [any of] my people [that is] poor by thee, thou shalt not be to him as an usurer, neither shalt thou lay upon him usury."*

Leviticus 25:37 *"Thou shalt not give him thy money upon usury, nor lend him thy victuals for increase."*

Deut. 15:6 *"For the Lord thy God blesseth thee, as he promised thee: and thou shalt lend unto many nations, but thou shalt not borrow; and thou shalt reign over many nations, but they shall not reign over thee."*

Deut. 23:19 *"Thou shalt not lend upon usury to thy brother; usury of money, usury of victuals, usury of any thing that is lent upon usury."*

Deut. 24:10 *"When thou dost lend thy brother any thing, thou shalt not go into his house to fetch his pledge."*

Luke 6:34 *"And if ye lend [to them] of whom ye hope to receive, what thank have ye? For sinners also lend to sinners, to receive as much again."*

Luke 6:35 *"But love ye your enemies, and do good, and lend, hoping for nothing again; and your reward shall be great, and ye shall be the children of the Highest: for he is kind unto the unthankful and [to] the evil."*

Punishment
Should the hands of thieves be cut off?

Matthew 5:30 states: *"And if thy right hand offend thee, cut it off, and cast it from thee: for it is profitable for thee that one of thy members should perish, and not [that] thy whole body should be cast into hell."*

If you son is rebellious and a drunkard, should he be stoned to death?

Duet 21:1-21 states *"If a man have a stubborn and rebellious son, which will not obey the voice of his father, or the voice of his mother, and [that], when they have chastened him, will not hearken unto them: Then shall his father and his mother lay hold on him, and bring him out unto the elders of his city, and unto the gate of his place; And they shall say unto the elders of his city, This our son [is] stubborn and rebellious, he will not obey our voice; [he is] a glutton, and a drunkard. And all the men of his city shall stone him with stones, that he dies: so shalt thou put evil away from among you; and all Israel shall hear, and fear."*

Should anyone who serves or worships anything or anyone except The God Of Israel be stoned to death? What about Christians who worship Christ?

Deut. 17: 3-5 says *"He that hath gone and served other gods, and worshipped them, either the sun, or moon, or any of the host of heaven, which I have not commanded; And it be told thee, and thou hast heard [of it], and inquired diligently, and, behold, [it be] true, [and] the thing certain, [that] such abomination is wrought in Israel: Then shalt thou bring forth that man or that woman, which have committed that wicked thing, unto thy gates, [even] that man or that woman, and shalt stone them with stones, till they die."*

Should a woman be executed if she is not a virgin when she gets married?

Duet: 22:20-21 says she should. *"But if this thing be true, [and the tokens of] virginity be not found for the damsel: Then they shall bring out the damsel to the door of her father's house, and the men of her city shall stone her with stones that she die: because she hath wrought folly in Israel, to play the whore in her father's house: so shalt thou put evil away from among you."*

And why is it that the young woman who is not a virgin gets stoned to death but the man who took her virginity can go free?

Should those who commit adultery be executed?

Deut: 22:22 *"If a man be found lying with a woman married to a husband, then they shall both of them die, [both] the man that lay with the woman, and the woman: so shalt thou put away evil from Israel. "* Ezek 23:47 *"And the company shall stone them with stones, and dispatch them with their swords; they shall slay their sons and their daughters, and burn up their houses with fire."*

Are we commanded to kill those who practice witchcraft?

"Exd 22:18 *"Thou shalt not suffer a witch to live."*

Certainly they took this serious in the Middle Ages with their witch burnings.

If a friend or family member invites you to consider any religion other than Judaism, should that person be killed?

Deut 13:6-10 says *"If thy brother, the son of thy mother, or thy son, or thy daughter, or the wife of thy bosom, or thy friend, which [is] as thine own soul, entice thee secretly, saying, Let us go and serve other gods, which thou hast not known, thou, nor thy fathers; Namely, of the gods of the people which [are] round about you, nigh unto thee, or far off from thee, from the [one] end of the earth even unto the [other] end of the earth; Thou shalt not consent unto him, nor hearken unto him; neither shall thine eye pity him, neither shalt thou spare, neither shalt thou conceal him: But thou shalt surely kill him; thine hand shall be first upon him to put him to death, and afterwards the hand of all the people. And thou shalt stone him with stones, that he die; because he hath sought to thrust thee away from the Lord thy God, which brought thee out of the land of Egypt, from the house of bondage. "*

Should those who work on Saturday (the seventh day/Sabbath) be put to death?

Exd 35:2 states clearly "Six days shall work be done, but on the seventh day there shall be to you an holy day, a Sabbath of rest to the Lord: whosoever doeth work therein shall be put to death."

That one catches most Christians.

Is Jesus "God"?
Matthew 19:17 & Mark 10:18 A man approached Jesus and addressed him as "Good Master" to which he replied:

"And he said unto him, Why callest thou me good? There is none good but one, that is, God."

In this passage from both Matthew and Mark, he clearly makes a distinction between himself and God.

Animal Sacrifice
Does God demand animal sacrifice? What kind of God is pleased by the smell of burning flesh or demands blood to be satisfied? Does this sound like the Creator of the Universe or some kind of tribal cult?

In Exodus 20:24, God commands that *"An altar of earth thou shalt make unto me, and shalt sacrifice thereon thy burnt offerings, and thy peace offerings, thy sheep, and thine oxen: in all places where I record my name I will come unto thee, and I will bless thee."*

Leviticus 1:14 states *"And if the burnt sacrifice for his offering to the Lord be of fowls, then he shall bring his offering of turtledoves, or of young pigeons."*

Actually most of Leviticus 3, 4 & 7 are about animal sacrifice.

Drinking Poison & Handling Poisonous Snakes
If one is a true Christian then, according to Mark 16:17-18 he can drink poison and handle poisonous snakes and this won't harm him.

"And these signs shall follow them that believe; In my name shall they cast out devils; they shall speak with new tongues; They shall take up serpents; and if they drink any deadly thing, it shall not hurt them; they shall lay hands on the sick, and they shall recover." (Mark 16:17-18).

So if you are a real Christian, you can drink arsenic and handle cobras and they won't hurt you, right? Haven't seen too many takers on that one!

Genocide
Does God condone and even promote genocide?

Deuteronomy 3:6 *"And we utterly destroyed them, as we did unto Sihon king of Heshbon, utterly destroying the men, women, and children, of every city."*

1Samuel 22:19 *"And Nob, the city of the priests, smote he with the edge of the sword, both men and women, children and sucklings, and oxen, and asses, and sheep, with the edge of the sword."*

Ezekiel 9:6 *"Slay utterly old and young, both maids, and little children, and women: but come not near any man upon whom is the mark; and begin at my sanctuary. Then they began at the ancient men which were before the house."*

Slavery
Does the bible condone slavery?

Exodus 21:7 states: *"And if a man sell his daughter to be a maidservant, she shall not go out as the menservants do."*

Ephesians 6:5 *"Servants, be obedient to them that are your masters according to the flesh, with fear and trembling, in singleness of your heart, as unto Christ;"*

Titus 2:9 *"Servants to be obedient unto their own masters, and to please them well in all things; not answering."*

Leviticus 25:44-45 *"Slaves, male and female, you may indeed possess, provided you buy them from among the neighboring nations. You may also buy them from among the aliens who reside with you and from their children who are born and reared in your land. Such slaves you may own as chattels and leave to your sons as their hereditary property, making them perpetual slaves."*

Slavery in the "Christian Nation" of the USA...

1680: The Anglican Church in Virginia started a debate that lasted for 50 years, on whether slaves should be given Christian instruction. They finally decided in the affirmative. However the landowners and slave owners opposed this program. They feared that if the slaves became Christians, there would be public support to recognizing them as full human beings and to grant them freedom.

In the predominately 'Christian' America, slaves were considered property and were not allowed to marry. The courts decided that a slave owner should be free to sell his property as he wished.

This overturned laws that prevented slave families from being broken up and the individuals sold separately.

Throughout most of the colonial period, opposition to slavery among white Americans was virtually nonexistent. Settlers in the 17th and early 18th centuries came from sharply stratified societies in which the wealthy savagely exploited members of the lower classes. Lacking a later generation's belief in natural human equality, they saw little reason to question the enslavement of Africans.

All of this of course was conveniently justified by biblical passages, both old and New Testament, of which there were plenty.

It is also important to note that not only slavery but other atrocities such as burning heretics at the stake for believing the Earth was round instead of flat (as scripture would indicate in Ezekiel 7:2 and again in Isaiah 11:12 where it speaks of the 'four corners of the Earth) or teaching that the Earth is over 6,000 years old, as the linage from Adam to Christ would indicate...all of this - the unspeakable torture and burnings of 'heretics' was done at the behest of 'good Christian clergy' - based on biblical passages - who were fully convinced that they were right and the rest of the world was wrong.

Something to think about, isn't it?

Here is something else to think about? What exactly did Jesus mean when he said - in Matthew 5:39 - "Resist not evil?" Or what did he mean when he said, in Luke 6: 27-36, "Love Your Enemies? Does this only refer to individuals? What about "Christian" presidents leading a nation to war to "fight evil" and to kill your enemies? How can a soldier be a Christian?

Again, something to think about.

Fantasy enthusiasts will love this. Dragons do exist! – At least according to the King James version of the bible. Check it out:

Job 30: 29-31: *"I am a brother to dragons, and a companion to owls. My skin is black upon me, and my bones are burned with heat. My harp also is turned to mourning, and my organ into the voice of them that weep."*

Isaiah 27:1: *"In that day the Lord with his hard and great and strong sword will punish Leviathan the fleeing serpent, Leviathan the twisting serpent, and he will slay the dragon that is in the sea."*

Isaiah 51:9: *"Awake, awake, put on strength, O arm of the Lord; awake, as in days of old, the generations of long ago. Was it not you who cut Rahab in pieces, who pierced the dragon?"*

Ezekiel 32:2: *"Son of man, raise a lamentation over Pharaoh king of Egypt and say to him: 'You consider yourself a lion of the nations, but you are like a dragon in the seas; you burst forth in your rivers, trouble the waters with your feet, and foul their rivers."*

Psalm 91:13: *"Thou shalt tread upon the lion and adder: the young lion and the dragon shalt thou trample under feet."*

Revelation 12:9: *"And the great dragon was thrown down, that ancient serpent, who is called the devil and Satan, the deceiver of the whole world—he was thrown down to the earth, and his angels were thrown down with him."*

Revelation 13:1-18: *"And I saw a beast rising out of the sea, with ten horns and seven heads, with ten diadems on its horns and blasphemous names on its heads. And the beast that I saw was like a leopard; its feet were like a bear's, and its mouth was like a lion's mouth. And to it the dragon gave his power and his throne and great authority. One of its heads seemed to have a mortal wound, but its mortal wound was healed, and the whole earth marveled as they followed the beast. And they worshiped the dragon, for he had given his authority to the beast, and they worshiped the beast, saying, "Who is like the beast, and who can fight against it?" And the beast was given a mouth uttering haughty and blasphemous words, and it was allowed to exercise authority for forty-two months."*

Revelation 20:2: *"And he seized the dragon, that ancient serpent, who is the devil and Satan, and bound him for a thousand years."*

Revelation 16:13: "And I saw, coming out of the mouth of the dragon and out of the mouth of the beast and out of the mouth of the false prophet, three unclean spirits like frogs."

Revelation 12:3: *"And another sign appeared in heaven: behold, a great red dragon, with seven heads and ten horns, and on his heads seven diadems."*

The Ten Commandments

Exodus 20:4: "Thou shalt not make unto thee any graven image, or any likeness of any thing that is in heaven above, or that is in the earth beneath, or that is in the water under the earth"

If we take this literally, then are those with photo albums or pictures hanging on their walls are sinners? And Kodak and all the camera companies are in sinful businesses?

Exodus 20:8: *"Remember the Sabbath day, to keep it holy. Six days shalt thou labor, and do all thy work, but the seventh day is the Sabbath of the Lord thy God. In it thou shalt not do any work, thou, nor thy son, nor thy daughter, thy manservant, nor thy maidservant, nor thy cattle, nor thy stranger that is within thy gates."*

Sabbath in Hebrew is Seventh - the seventh day - Saturday. So those who work on Saturday or allow their families or others who serve them to work on Saturday, have broken this commandment, right?

Exodus 20"13 *"Thou shalt not kill."* Exodus 20:15: *"Thou shalt not steal."*

Now this is interesting one. It really doesn't say "kill what..." or steal from whom? I've yet to find anyone who takes these literally. Certainly Jews, Christians and Muslims don't

In common practice, the rule of thumb seems to be that you shouldn't kill or steal within your own family, tribe, ethnic group or country. It's OK to kill animals, forests, foreigners, and those who break social norms or don't accept your religion or politics. And it's OK to steal the land and resources of foreigners through conquest and occupation.

Oh, and here is the kicker. There is nothing in the bible that says you should go to church on Sunday, and there are over 100 passages in the bible that refer to gluttony. Wow! That can put a damper on your all-you-can-eat buffet outing!

And the list goes on and on...

Of course there are those who might explain away many of the verses, especially those in the Old Testament. But can one accept some commandments or teachings from the Old Testament and not others? Can one only accept those which are convenient or which back up ones' prejudices or preconceived notions? In the book of James 2:10 it says "For whoever keeps the whole law but fails in one point has become guilty of all of it."

This is not to take away from the essence of the teachings of Jesus or even the bible as a whole, but it is to say that one must consider all of these matters in their historic & cultural context. Throughout history the church has used the bible teachings to justify such things as

* Torture
* Burning people at the stake,
* The buying and selling of slaves
* Stoning people to death
* Invading and conquering countries and committing unspeakable atrocities
... to name a few.

The Bible contains many books by many different authors over a very long period of history. It is easy to find passages to justify virtually anything. For those who are fond of quoting the bible, I would ask, which bible? There are 21 English version of the bible currently in use, including 3 versions of King James.

Versions of the Bible
* 21st Century King James Version
* Amplified Bible
* American Standard Version
* Contemporary English Version
* Darby Translation
* English Standard Version
* Holman Christian Standard Bible
* King James Version
* New American Standard Bible
* New Living Translation
* New King James Version
* New Century Version
* New International
* New International Reader's Version
* New Life Version
* New International Version – UK

* Today's New Testament Version
* The Message
* Wycliffe New Testament
* World Wide English New Testament
* Young's Literal Translation

Which is correct? King James, you say? Which version of the King James (there are three). The King James version is a translation of a translation of a translation produced in 1611 with wording that was common in the Elizabethan era of England. Some of the more recent translations were made from the original Greek, which show differences in meaning in some passages than the King James version. Which is correct and why?

English Bible History
If you are seriously interested in the subject, check this out: www.greatsite.com/timeline-english-bible-history. It is a timeline of how we got the English bible.

An interesting side note that few people know is the fact that "King James" was actually gay... Really. It was a well-known fact during his time. http://wiki.answers.com/Q/Was_king_james_gay

My Personal Journey of Faith
In my 20's I was a very conservative and I will have to say a "narrow-minded" Christian. I struggled very hard to do what I thought the bible taught. Like the Pharisees that Jesus spoke of, I was self-righteous and judgmental (of myself and others) focusing on the rules and intricate wording of the teachings and totally missing the spirit of those teachings - which is Love.

I am now nearing 70. When people ask me if I am a Christian, I say "which kind are you referring to: an "about" Christian or an "of" Christian?" The former are those who believe all or many of the multiple different teachings 'about' Jesus according to the 38,000 different Christian denominations in the world today. The second are those who believe and endeavor to follow the very simple teachings "of" Jesus. No, I am not an 'about' Christian. And yes, I am an "of" Christian which also puts me in resonance with the highest and deepest teachings of all of the great masters and teachers.

But more importantly, I am totally at peace with God and with myself. I live a life of total Gratitude for all the grace that fills my life. I did not have any of this when I was an 'about' Christian.

I am not opposed to the church. It does many good things and serves as a vital vehicle for many, as it did for me at one point in my life. But for me it was "spiritual kindergarten." As I grew spiritually and developed an intimate relationship with Divine Presence, I grew out of and away from organized religion. That has been my path. It may not be for everyone. We are all different and are at different points in souls' journey.

The planet Earth and her inhabitants are moving into uncharted territory. I have traveled around the world and seen organized religion in all of its different forms. By and large I have found organized religion to be largely a museum of cultural beliefs which existed at the time of its founding and which have been enshrined with spiritual authority. This doesn't make it bad. There is a place for museums. But they are tail lights of the human experience. Generally they don't serve as headlights leading us into a new era – and especially into uncharted territory.

Having said all of that, I will say that for me personally, there is only one central teaching. That is where Jesus said, "all of the laws and commandments are summed up in this one law; love God with all your heart, mind and soul, and your neighbor as yourself." I figure that my efforts to perfect this one could take a few hundred more lifetimes.

The human heart is the one temple, church, mosque, synagogue and shrine that we all share in common. This is the one place we can all meet Divine Presence and one another in Unity and Oneness.

Recommended Reading
The following are a few of the books that have significantly impacted my own life. If you are interested in additional selections, just contact me at lightweave@aol.com If you are not a reader, you may find some good videos on YouTube by the same authors.

Jonathan Livingston Seagull (Richard Bach)
"Most gulls don't bother to learn more than the simplest facts of flight--how to get from shore to food and back again," writes author Richard Bach in this allegory about a unique bird named Jonathan Livingston Seagull. "For most gulls it is not flying that matters, but eating. For this gull, though, it was not eating that mattered, but flight." Ultimately this is a fable about the importance of seeking a higher purpose in life, even if your flock, tribe, or neighborhood finds your ambition threatening. By not compromising his higher vision, Jonathan gets the ultimate payoff: transcendence. Ultimately, he learns the meaning of love and kindness.

As A Man Thinketh (James Allen)

James Allen said that a person's mind is like a garden, which may be intelligently cultivated, or allowed to run wild. Either way, the garden will bring forth. You will be awed by the relevance of the author's thoughts and observations on the power of the mind, and mankind's ability to control life's outcomes by controlling what goes into it. This is a gift book that every pilgrim receives as a companion for their journey.

The Way Out (Joseph Benner)

The Way Out helps the reader come to terms with the source of their life challenges to ultimately achieve and prosper from the deep level of the soul. As the author writes, "Whatever you think and hold in consciousness as being so, manifests itself in your body or affairs." Whether you accept this or not, consider for a while the truth that every thought you think, especially those

relating in any way to self, hovers around in your mental atmosphere just as a child stays close to its parent. These thoughts being about yourself receive the life that maintains them from the feeling that you put into them.

Psycho Cybernetics 2000 (Maltz)

Rather than relying on the Freudian approach of yielding control to the subconscious or on "will power" to change behavior, Psycho-Cybernetics (a computer term referring to the mental "steering system" that guides our attitudes, behavior and self-image) directs the intuitive and nonverbal right brain to "reprogram" the logical and verbal left brain through a six-step program. The steps are: programming your "success mechanism," imagining success, shedding false beliefs, learning to relax, using "drug-free tranquilizers" and setting goals. The author shows how people have improved their self-images and have realized their goals using Maltz's program. Self-quizzes are included.

Success Through Positive Mental Attitude (W. Stone)

PMA stands for "positive mental attitude." This is the foundation that best selling author, Napoleon Hill based his teachings of motivation to millions of people who have transformed their lives for the better. Hill went from living in a log cabin to the life of a millionaire and influence as the author of internationally acclaimed best sellers and adviser to heads of state. This was all made possible by living what he taught.

Keys To Success (Napoleon Hill)

Hill's seventeen essential principles of personal achievement are expanded on in detail, with concrete advice on their use and implementation. You will learn the

secrets of:
* filling your life with purpose and direction
* perfecting your personality
* fanning your creative spark
* building self-discipline
* profiting from the Golden Rule
* budgeting time and money
* discovering and preserving the source of all wealth

Real Magic - Creating Miracles In Everyday Life (Wayne Dyer)

"Real magic," according to Dyer, has nothing to do with sorcerers or fairy godmothers. It occurs in our daily lives when we let go of negativity and self-limiting beliefs about ourselves and our circumstances . Dyer offers concrete suggestions about how to "get to purpose" through service to others and unconditional love, how to become spiritual beings and how to create a "miracle mindset." He also explores ways readers might improve relationships and find prosperity, personal identity and even physical health. Finally, he explains how "real magic" can be plumbed on the global level to alleviate world problems.

The 7 Habits of Highly Effective People (Stephen Covey)

In The 7 Habits of Highly Effective People, Covey presents a holistic, integrated, principle-centered approach for solving personal and professional problems. With penetrating insights and pointed anecdotes, Covey reveals a step-by-step pathway for living with fairness, integrity, service, and human dignity -- principles that give us the security to adapt to change and the wisdom and power to take advantage of the opportunities that change creates.

The Law Of Attraction (Michael Losier)

You're already experiencing the Law of Attraction. You may not be aware of it, but this powerful force is at work in your life, attracting people, situations and relationships. This book will teach you how to make the Law of Attraction work for you by helping you eliminate the unwanted from your life and filling it up with the things that give you energy, prosperity and joy.

You can use the Law of Attraction to make a few changes in your life or do a complete overhaul. You'll find all the tools in this book. Discover how easy it is to use the Law of Attraction to: stop attracting things you don't want, increase wealth, find your perfect mate, clarify your goals and strategies, and locate your ideal job.

Goals!
How To Get Everything you Want Faster Than You Ever Thought Possible (Brian Tracy)
Based on more than 20 years of experience and 40 years of research, this book presents a practical, proven strategy for creating and meeting goals that has been used by more than 1 million people to achieve extraordinary things in life. Author Brian Tracy explains the seven key elements of goal setting and the 12 steps necessary to set and accomplish goals of any size. Using simple language and real-life examples, Tracy shows how to do the crucial work of determining one's strengths, values, and true goals. He explains how to build the self-esteem and confidence necessary for achievement; how to overpower every problem or obstacle; how to overcome difficulties; how to respond to challenges; and how to continue moving forward no matter what happens. The book's "Mental Fitness" program of character development shows readers how to become the kind of person on the inside who can achieve any goal on the outside.

Living Life as a Thank You: The Transformative Power of Daily Gratitude (Mary Beth Sammons)
Whatever is given — even a difficult and challenging moment — is a gift. Living as if each day is a thank-you can help transform fear into courage, anger into forgiveness, isolation into belonging, and another's pain into healing. Saying thank-you every day inspires feelings of love, compassion, and hope. In this timely book the authors present a simple, but comprehensive program for incorporating gratitude into one's life, and reaping the many benefits that come from doing so.

The book is divided into ten chapters from "Thank You Power" and "Ways to Stay Thankful in Difficult Times" to "Gratitude as a Spiritual/Cultural Practice " and "Putting Gratitude into Action." Each chapter includes stories of individuals whose lives have been transformed by embracing this program, along with motivating quotes and blessings, and a suggested gratitude practice such as keeping a weekly gratitude journal and starting a gratitude circle.

Nonviolent Communication: A Language Of Life (Marshall Rosenberg)
Do you hunger for skills to improve the quality of your relationships, to deepen your sense of personal empowerment or to simply communicate more effectively? Unfortunately, for centuries our culture has taught us to think and speak in ways that can actually perpetuate conflict, internal pain and even violence. Nonviolent Communication offers practical skills with a powerful consciousness and vocabulary to help you get what you want peacefully.

Rosenberg offers insightful stories, anecdotes, practical exercises and role-plays that will dramatically change your approach to communication for the better. Discover how the language you use can strengthen your relationships, build trust, prevent conflicts and heal pain. Revolutionary, yet simple, NVC offers you the most effective tools to reduce violence and create peace in your life-one interaction at a time.

How To Win Friends & Influence People (Dale Carnegie)
This grandfather of all people-skills books was first published in 1937. It was an overnight hit, eventually selling 15 million copies. How to Win Friends and Influence People is just as useful today as it was when it was first published, because Dale Carnegie had an understanding of human nature that will never be outdated. Financial success, Carnegie believed, is due 15 percent to professional knowledge and 85 percent to "the ability to express ideas, to assume leadership, and to arouse enthusiasm among people." He teaches these skills through underlying principles of dealing with people so that they feel important and appreciated. He also emphasizes fundamental techniques for handling people without making them feel manipulated.

Carnegie says you can make someone want to do what you want them to by seeing the situation from the other person's point of view and "arousing in the other person an eager want." You learn how to make people like you, win people over to your way of thinking, and change people without causing offense or arousing resentment.

For instance, "let the other person feel that the idea is his or hers," and "talk about your own mistakes before criticizing the other person." Carnegie illustrates his points with anecdotes of historical figures, leaders of the business world, and everyday folks

Loving What Is:
Four Questions That Can Change Your Life (Byron Katie)
Out of nowhere, like a breeze in a marketplace crowded with advice, comes Byron Katie and "The Work." In the midst of a normal life, Katie became increasingly depressed, and over a ten-year period sank further into rage, despair, and thoughts of suicide. Then one morning, she woke up in a state of absolute joy, filled with the realization of how her own suffering had ended. The freedom of that realization has never left her, and now in Loving What Is you can discover the same freedom through The Work.

The Work is simply four questions that, when applied to a specific problem, enable you to see what is troubling you in an entirely different light. As Katie says, "It's not the problem that causes our suffering; it's our thinking about the problem." Contrary to popular belief, trying to let go of a painful thought never works; instead, once we have done The Work, the thought lets go of us. At that point, we can truly love what is, just as it is.

Journey of Souls:
Case Studies Of Life Between Lives (Michael Newton)
Learn the latest details and most recent groundbreaking discoveries that reveal, for the first time, the mystery of life in the spirit world after death on Earth — proof that our consciousness survives. Using a special hypnosis technique to reach the hidden memories of subjects, Dr. Newton discovered some amazing insights into what happens to us between lives. *Journey of Souls* is the record of 29 people who recalled their experiences between physical deaths. Through their extraordinary stories, you will learn specifics about:
·How it feels to die · What you see and feel right after death · The truth about "spiritual guides" · What happens to "disturbed" souls · Why you are assigned to certain soul groups in the spirit world · How you choose another body to return to Earth · The different levels of souls: beginning, intermediate, and advanced ·When and where you first learn to recognize soul mates on Earth · The purpose of life

Journey of Souls is a graphic record or "travel log" by these people of what happens between lives on Earth. They give specific details as they movingly describe their astounding experiences.

After reading *Journey of Souls,* you will gain a better understanding of the immortality of the human soul. You will meet day-to-day challenges with a greater sense of purpose. You will begin to understand the reasons behind events in your own life.

Tao Te Ching & Hua Hu Ching (Translation by Brian Walker)
The Tao Te Ching of Lao Tzu is among the most widely translated and cherished books in the world. Singular in its lucidity, revered across cultural boundaries for its timeless wisdom, it is believed among Westerners to be Lao Tzu's only book. Few are aware that a collection of his oral teachings on the subject of attaining enlightenment and mastery were also recorded in a book called the Hua Hu Ching The teachings of the Hua Hu Ching are of genuine power and consequence, a road map to the divine realm for ordinary human beings.

Brian Browne Walker's contemporary translations of Taoist classics have received high marks for their simplicity, clarity, and accessibility.

Mountain Light Community Prayer

Divine Presence
Whose Nature Is Love
Let me be an instrument of your peace;
Where there is hatred, let me bring love;
Where there is doubt, let me bring faith;
Where there is sadness, let me bring joy;
Where there is fear, let me bring courage;
Where there is despair, let me bring hope;
Where there is illness, let me bring health;
Where there is darkness, let me bring light;
Where there is lack, let me bring abundance;
Where there is discord, let me bring harmony;
Where there is bondage, let me bring freedom;
Where there is ignorance, let me bring wisdom;
Where there is injury, let me bring forgiveness;
Where there is weakness, let me bring strength;
Where there is poverty, let me bring prosperity;
Where the is suffering, let me bring compassion;

May I always remember to treat others
As I myself wish to be treated;
To understand others more than to be understood;
To love more than to be loved;
For I know that it is in giving that we receive,
It is by forgiving that we are forgiven
And it is in rising above duality
That we are awakened into Oneness
Amen

Adapted From the prayer of St. Francis of Assisi

Mountain Light Sanctuary
www.mtnlightsanctuary.com

65424096R00063

Made in the USA
Lexington, KY
12 July 2017